Unleash The Millionaire Within

34 Exercises To Unleash Your Potential
And Finally Win The Game of Money

Published by

Inspired Publishing Ltd
27 Old Gloucester Street
London
WC1N 3AX

inspiredpublishing

Printed in the United Kingdom

ISBN: 978-1-78555-056-0

DEDICATION

This book is dedicated to the thousands of clients and seminar attendees I have met all over the world since I began this journey. Thank you for all your support. I am privileged to have been a part of your story so far. You continue to inspire me.

Table of Contents

INTRODUCTION

"Making money is so easy!" sniggered Balthazar, as he tilted his head back and let out a laugh. He had just made thousands of pounds from his desk, for less than ten minutes "work". The Internet had changed everything.

I was at his home because I needed a mentor, but in that moment only rage filled my thoughts. "How DARE you say that making money is EASY?! Making money is HARD! Everyone knows that! My father was always broke... my grandparents too... I have always been broke... we ALWAYS struggled financially... that's real life! You have no idea!"

That's what I was *thinking*, as my blood boiled, but said nothing. It's a good thing he had his back to me in that moment or he would have noticed me glaring at him.

We had met at a seminar a couple of weeks prior. I had offered to work for him for free, in exchange for him teaching me what he knew about wealth and success.

When he was done at his computer, he came over and sat across from me on the couch, in the ornately decorated office he'd set up in his palatial home on the outskirts of London.

"So..." he began, jovially. "What is your goal? What do you want to achieve?"

I began to cry. "I… I just want to be DEBT-FREE!" I stuttered, as I put my head in my hands. "I am £7,000 in debt!"

As a security guard, in my early twenties, I had been earning just £3.25 an hour before becoming unemployed. With such low earnings, this debt seemed insurmountable and felt suffocating.

"That's IT? That's ALL you want to achieve?! You have no other ambition than to pay off a measly few thousand?!" he erupted. "You know what your problem is? You are not adding any real VALUE! You are not solving problems for people. You are not PRODUCING anything of value. Go out there and start HELPING people! THAT'S how money starts flowing to you! Money is nothing but the measure of the value you create for other people!"

I tried to remonstrate by explaining my situation but he cut me off: "If you are struggling to pay your bills, then you have a belief inside of you that says 'I must struggle'."

He continued: "Listen. There are seven steps to unleashing your financial potential. It starts by taking full responsibility for your results in life. And then getting crystal clear on exactly who you are and what you want."

Frustrated with the meek answers I offered up to his questions, he handed me a handful of printed pages of paper slid inside a musty old book, and stood up. I had used up his patience, it seemed.

His parting words were:

> "Complete these exercises and read this book. It contains the accumulated wisdom of a hundred great wealth builders. They call this the science of 'Wealth Magnetics'. It will teach you how to change your <u>thinking</u>. The magic it contains will magnetize wealth *to* you. Get in touch only when this is done."

And with that, he showed me to the door.

* * * * * * * * *

The words of this most peculiar man were still ringing in my ears as I made my way back to the city, wondering...

"What does he mean, the magic it contains will magnetize wealth to me?!"

* * * * * * * * *

On the train ride I dusted off the book Balthazar had given me and opened it to a random page.

"When you adopt this secret mindset, things just fall into place perfectly, money flows to you from unexpected places, and the right opportunities are attracted to you as if by magic...", it read, intriguingly.

Little did I know at the time, but less than a month later I would be earning $10,000 a month in passive income from my first ever business.

This chance encounter with Balthazar would represent a turning point in my life; a catalyst to greater things. It opened up my mind to ideas I would have never, ever come across under normal circumstances. Today, I, in turn, invite <u>you</u>, the reader, to think bigger than you've ever thought before. Your potential is limitless.

* * * * * * * * *

Sometimes when we pray for a solution to our problems, the answer doesn't come in the form of "a bag of cash falling out of the sky"—that would be too easy, wouldn't it? —but in the shape of **an opportunity to gain wisdom and elevate our thinking.** We can't solve problems by using the same kind of thinking we used when we created them, as Albert Einstein once said.

This is why I had put together the last remaining credit on my eighth and final credit card to pay to attend that personal development seminar. I hadn't received a paycheck since getting fired from my job six months prior. Asking my parents back home for cash was out of the question. They didn't have money, they didn't know I was homeless, they were going through a nasty divorce, and besides, they had enough to worry about. It didn't help that I hadn't spoken to my father in 5 years, either.

3

That amount—£300—was enough money for me to live on *for two whole months*. But I rationalized that since attending a seminar was the sort of thing I would never do or spend money on normally—and all my previous decisions had brought me to this point of total destitution—this *had* to be a good idea.

The twenty or so homeless people that shared the building with me—we were squatting it illegally—thought I was crazy. Ever had a homeless person think you are crazy?

"You're going to lose your money. These things never work. What? You think you can change your life? Wake up! Who do you think you are anyway?!" they kept saying.

"What have I got to lose?" I thought to myself. "Even if I only get ONE good idea that can change my life, it's worth the investment!"

* * * * * * * *

It was late in the evening when I got to London. The usual bustle of bleary-eyed workers heading home and last-minute shoppers filled the streets, as the grey, overcast sky gave way to nightfall.

I had refused to get on the dole and receive "unemployment benefits." The idea of submitting myself to the government in order to receive a pittance of £240 a month was anathema to me. I was homeless, I was unemployed, but I was free.

"At least now I have all the time in the world to read this book and do these exercises…" I thought to myself with a chuckle.

And with that I began going over Balthazar's exercises, as I sat on the cold, concrete floor, paper and pen in hand.

* * * * * * * *

CHAPTER 1

Clarity Is Power

I began immersing myself in an intense process of self-analysis, while reading Balthazar's book. The ideas jumped off the page at me fast and furious. *Know thyself* advocated Socrates. *The first and greatest victory is to conquer yourself*, wrote Plato. *To thine own self be true*, urged Shakespeare.

It is nigh impossible to be true to oneself when you don't know yourself, of course, and so often nowadays people's innate values and purpose have been subverted by parents' wishes or by the advertising industry's values portrayed in the media (placing a high importance on material things, status, wealth, fame). People no longer know who they really are.

What I quickly found out was that you get your life to take off by first becoming *very clear* about what you really want. **The clearer you are about what you want, the less time you waste chasing dead-ends and the faster you make your life goals happen.**

I believe that if you get absolutely crystal clear on exactly what you want to experience in your life, and you can't see anything *but* that in your mind's eye, it is almost impossible for you not to get it.

Knowing yourself can be one of the most stabilizing things you will ever do. This process begins with self-analysis and self-awareness.

EXERCISE #1 – SELF-AWARENESS

What things, activities, experiences, or people make you feel HAPPY?

_____

_____

_____

_____

_____

_____

_____

_____

_____

_____

_____

_____

_____

_____

_____

What things, activities, experiences, thoughts, habits, or people make you feel UNHAPPY?

_____

_____

_____

_____

_____

_____

_____

_____

_____

_____

_____

_____

_____

_____

_____

What are you currently upset about?

_____

_____

_____

_____

_____

_____

_____

What are you currently anxious about?

_____

_____

_____

_____

_____

_____

_____

_____

(Tip: Do MORE of what makes you feel happy. Do LESS of what makes you unhappy. Obvious, right?)

What has to happen in order for you to feel happy? What are your "rules" for allowing yourself to be happy?

_____

_____

_____

_____

_____

_____

_____

What has to happen in order for you to feel successful?

_____

_____

_____

_____

_____

_____

_____

_____

Set yourself up for happiness: What could your *new* rules for happiness be? Complete this sentence: *"I feel happy whenever…"*

_____

_____

_____

_____

_____

_____

_____

_____

"I feel successful whenever…"

_____

_____

_____

_____

_____

_____

_____

_____

"You get your life to "take off" by first becoming very clear in your thinking about it. You can't expect God to be less clear than you, and so produce it for you. Think about what you want to be, do, and have. Think about it often until you are very clear about this. Then, when you are very clear, think about nothing else. Imagine no other possibilities. Throw all negative thoughts out of your mental constructions. Lose all pessimism. Release all doubts. Reject all fears. Discipline your mind to hold fast to the original creative thought."

Neale Donald Walsch, *Conversations With God*

EXERCISE #2 – DISCOVER YOUR PURPOSE

Answering the following questions will help you identify your life purpose:

❑ What do you love talking about when you meet up with friends? What do you love talking about at barbeques, or social settings? What do people keep asking you about at parties?

_____

_____

_____

_____

_____

_____

_____

❑ What do you love doing in your spare time? What are your favourite pastimes or hobbies?

_____

_____

_____

_____

❑ What problem do you love solving for people?

_____

_____

_____

_____

_____

❑ Complete this sentence: "I really enjoy helping people with…"

_____

_____

_____

_____

❑ Complete this sentence: "I feel fulfilled when I help people…"

_____

_____

_____

_____

_____

❑ What are you passionate about? What makes you feel EXCITED?

_____

_____

_____

_____

_____

❑ What do you *hate?* What do you find yourself ranting *against?*

_____

_____

_____

_____

_____

❑ If you had $20m in the bank and you *knew* you could not fail, what would you be doing right now? *What would you love to create?*

_____

_____

_____

_____

_____

_____

❑ What would you say to the world if your five-minute message could reach everyone on the planet?

_____

_____

_____

_____

_____

❑ What is the title of the book you would love to write?

_____

_____

_____

❑ What is the title of the seminar, workshop, or retreat you would love to create and run?

_____

_____

_____

❑ What comes easy to you that is harder for others?

_____

_____

_____

❏ Think back to a scene from a movie that brought tears to your eyes. These moments can be *clues* as to what your life purpose really is. (Personally, I always cry when I watch the 'Gandhi' movie… the moment when Ghandi goes on hunger strike until the fighting between the Muslims and the Hindus stops…).

_____

_____

_____

_____

_____

❏ Complete the sentence: *"When I'm finally living my purpose I will…"*

_____

_____

_____

_____

_____

❏ Complete the sentence: *"I will know I have found my passion and I'm living the life of my dreams when I…"*

_____

_____

_____

_____

❑ Complete the sentence: *"When I'm following my passion I feel..."*

_____

_____

_____

❑ Complete the sentence: *"It is important to find my passion and live it because..."*

_____

_____

_____

❑ What would you have to BELIEVE about yourself in order to live a passionate life that you LOVE? Complete the sentence: *"In order to make my passion happen I would have to believe..."*

_____

_____

_____

❑ What is your inner voice—your intuition, your higher self— telling you that you should do?

_____

_____

_____

_____

17

❑ What advice would the future 'you' already living a passionate life, give to the present you?

_____

_____

_____

_____

_____

❑ When was the last time you were in a state of flow? What were you doing?

_____

_____

_____

_____

❑ If you only had 3 years to live, what would you do?

_____

_____

_____

_____

_____

❏ If you only had 12 months to live, what would you do?

_____

_____

_____

_____

_____

❏ If you only had 6 months to live, what would you do?

_____

_____

_____

_____

❏ If you only had 30 days to live, what would you do?

_____

_____

_____

_____

_____

❑ What prevents you from living the life of your dreams? What are you afraid of?

_____

_____

_____

_____

_____

❑ How could you take the next step towards your ideal life?

_____

_____

_____

_____

❑ "How can I do what I love and be magnificently paid for it?"

_____

_____

_____

_____

EXERCISE #3 – WRITE DOWN YOUR "MISSION STATEMENT"

Which of these 'mission statements' inspire you the most? (Tick three or four of them that resonate with you the most).

"To Unite People & Promote Equality." – Martin Luther King

"I shall not submit to injustice from anyone. I shall conquer untruth by truth." – Mahatma Gandhi

"To contribute to the making of a just society... a democratic and free society in which all persons live together in harmony and with equal opportunities." – Nelson Mandela

"A world without war." – John Lennon

"To help people achieve their goals faster and easier than ever before." – Brian Tracy

"To make a significant difference in the quality of life of people." – Anthony Robbins

"To elevate the financial wellbeing of our clients." – Robert Kiyosaki

"To help over 20 million people live meaningful lives with less." – Joshua Fields Millburn & Ryan Nicodemus, founders of 'TheMinimalists.com'

"To change people's lives for the better, by opening their mind to divinity." – Glyn Parry, 'The Miracle Man'

"To set up 100 healing centers around the world, to promote life-changing alternative medicine methods to the people who need it the most."

"To create the best organic food bistro that promotes healthy eating and sustainable agriculture."

"To help 10,000 abandoned or traumatized children live a life of meaning and joy."

21

"To help feed every month 100,000 destitute Greek people affected by the 'Financial Crisis'."

"To help millions of people re-discover their spirituality overcome depression."

"To help preserve wildlife habitats for endangered animals and for our future generations."

"To teach underprivileged children the keys to success and how they can change their life, and ignite their ambition."

"To help people dramatically improve their health and their quality of life in their old age."

"To eliminate 97% of diseases on our planet thanks to clean food, detoxification, and alternative medicine."

"To help people find the love of their lives, and make love come alive."

"To grow nutritious, organic food that helps people thrive and have vibrant health. To teach sustainable farming techniques that transform entire communities."

"To empower people to be self-sustaining by teaching them how to produce their own food, medicine, and power."

"To commercialize and make widely available 'Free Energy' technology; to empower people and eliminate the need for fossil fuels or nuclear power."

"To teach parents of autistic children how to reverse this condition through nutrition and detoxification."

"To raise awareness about how smoking has killed over 100,000,000 (one hundred million) people in the 20th century and drop the rate of new smokers by 50% worldwide."

"To create awesome sports and activity centers for young people, for them to have something to do in their spare time instead of turning to drugs and alcohol."

"To help people achieve their dream of being debt-free and owning their own home outright."

"To reduce teen suicides caused by bullying and a lack of self worth; to teach young people how to finally love themselves."

"To design and build wood desks and dining tables that make people happy and make people's homes more beautiful."

"To make people feel beautiful every day of their lives."

"To teach parents how to unleash their children's innate genius."

"To entertain people and make them laugh out loud!"

"To create extraordinary and unforgettable adventures for people in the most beautiful, exotic locations in the world."

"To help people break free from their dead-end jobs and discover what they really want to do with their lives."

What would YOUR mission statement be?

_____

_____

_____

_____

_____

EXERCISE #4 – SET YOUR GOALS

This is where you start creating your future—your new life, as you want it to be.

What are your financial goals?

"I earn _____ per month."

"I earn _____ per year."

"I have _____ in the bank."

"I have a net worth of _____"

"My business has achieved _____"

What are your relationship goals?

_____

_____

_____

_____

_____

_____

_____

What are your family-related goals?

_____

_____

_____

_____

_____

_____

_____

What are your health and fitness goals?

_____

_____

_____

_____

_____

_____

The Importance Of Having a Compelling Goal

"Where does ENERGY come from? Sleep? Food? NO! It comes from being excited! Having a compelling vision for your future! Having compelling goals that get you excited about getting up in the morning!"

Anthony Robbins

What do you want to create?

_____

_____

_____

_____

_____

_____

What experiences do you want to have?

_____

_____

_____

_____

_____

_____

What things do you want to own?

_____

_____

_____

_____

_____

_____

_____

Where do you want to live? (describe your ideal house or location)

_____

_____

_____

_____

_____

_____

_____

"Twenty years later, the 3% of Yale graduates with specific written goals had accumulated more financial wealth than the other 97% of the class combined."

Zig Ziglar

EXERCISE #5 – YOUR PERFECT LIFE SCRIPT

What does your ideal day look like? Describe your ideal day.

_____

_____

_____

_____

_____

_____

_____

_____

_____

_____

_____

_____

_____

_____

_____

_____

What does your ideal LIFE look like? Describe your ideal life, all the way to your 100th birthday.

_____

_____

_____

_____

_____

_____

_____

_____

_____

_____

_____

_____

_____

_____

_____

_____

_____

_____

_____

_____

_____

_____

_____

_____

_____

_____

_____

_____

_____

_____

_____

_____

_____

_____

_____

_____

"Write down what you want to do until you're 100 years old. Whatever I write down MANIFESTS, and what I leave out, others determine. That's why I spend hours and hours writing down how I want my life to be, in detail (it's a 400-page document now!). The people at the TOP of life spend hours planning and visualizing, and the people at the bottom... do it the least."

Dr. John Demartini

EXERCISE #6 – WHO DO YOU WANT TO BECOME?

This should be a critical part of your goal-setting process; deciding who you want to BE. Who is your ideal self? Here is an example of what I wrote years ago when I was broke and suffered from the most extreme levels of "low self-esteem" imaginable…

- ❑ I am disciplined
- ❑ I possess total self-confidence and self-mastery
- ❑ I am patient and perseverant
- ❑ I am positive, enthusiastic, passionate, committed!
- ❑ I never speak negatively of anyone
- ❑ I always smile at everyone and I walk tall
- ❑ I take excellent care of my health
- ❑ I am direct, candid, straightforward
- ❑ I have no need for approval
- ❑ I am solution-oriented
- ❑ I never complain nor express anger
- ❑ I am a leader
- ❑ I never give up on my dreams
- ❑ I am brave and unreasonable
- ❑ I never procrastinate and instead do things NOW
- ❑ I accept full responsibility for my life
- ❑ I express myself freely and creatively!
- ❑ I am amazing! I am inspiration! I am power!
- ❑ I love my life! I am rich, I am loved, I am grateful!
- ❑ I am a genius and I apply my wisdom!
- ❑ I inspire millions of people around the world!
- ❑ Every day, in every way, I am healthier & stronger!
- ❑ Every day in every way I am better & better!

Choose words from the list below that will describe the new YOU:

I Am Outstanding, Magnetic, Awesome, Sensual, Sexy, Inspirational, Charismatic, Confident, Phenomenal, Powerful, Strong, Invincible. Irrepressible, Unstoppable, Dynamic, Energetic, Unforgettable, Honest,

True, Creative, Sensational, Sublime, Joyful, Alive!, Passionate, Impulsive, Spontaneous, Warm, Natural, Kind, Caring, Compassionate, Fabulous, Stupendous!, Marvellous, Gorgeous, Fearless, Brave, Courageous, Talented, Highly Intelligent, Legendary, Unique, Enlightened, Free-spirited.

I Am a Leader, Visionary, Role-model, Free spirit, Guide, Teacher, Mentor, Legend, Motivator, Champion, Force For Good, Star!, Achiever, Maker of dreams, Creator of Magic, Millionaire, Master, Hero, Philosopher, Warrior, Poet, Icon, Entertainer, Innovator, Humanitarian.

I Am a Leader Who Achieves, Leads, Motivates, Envisions, Changes Lives, Creates, Gets results, Makes a difference, Communicates Vision, Inspires, Empowers, Educates, Discovers, Innovates, Enlightens, Gives & Contributes, Grows, Creates Magic, Rocks!, Lives Life To The Full!, Laughs & Has Fun, Takes Massive Action, Shines, Transforms, Defies All Odds, Touches lives, Revolutionizes, Persists, Conquers All, Unleashes the incredible potential of the Human spirit!

"Who I Am"

Drawing inspiration from the words and sentences in this section, describe the new 'you':

_____

_____

_____

_____

_____

_____

_____

_____

_____

_____

_____

_____

_____

_____

"You do not have to know the who, what, where, when and how what you want is going to happen. Your job is to be A CREATOR, to decree, to send out the blueprints into the fields of existence, and to do so consciously, with grace, with creativity, with bravado and courage, a little bit of humility... and GRATITUDE."

Barbara Marciniak

EXERCISE #7 – DISCOVER YOUR VALUES

This exercise, developed by Dr. John Demartini, is designed to help you identify your hierarchy of values. Understanding what is important to you (what you *value*) helps you prioritize what you want out of life, and can hint at what type of business or career you should be pursuing. It will also be of importance for subsequent exercises.

Fill in the answers to the following questions:

1. How do you fill your personal space?

Whatever you see around you in your home is a very strong clue as to what you value most. What three things fill your space the most?

_____

_____

_____

2. How do you spend your time?

People always make time for things that are really important to them and run out of time for things that aren't. How you spend your time tells you what matters to you most. In which three ways do *you* spend your time?

_____

_____

_____

3. How do you spend your energy?

You always have energy for things that you value most. You run out of energy for things that don't. In which three ways do you spend your energy and where do you feel energized?

_____

_____

_____

4. How do you spend your money?

You always find money for what is important to you. Your choices about spending money say a great deal about what you value most. In which three ways do you spend your money?

_____

_____

_____

5. Where do you have the most order in your life?

We tend to bring order and organization to things that are important to us and to allow chaos and disorder with things that are low on our values. In which three areas are you most organized?

_____

_____

_____

6. Where are you most reliable, disciplined, and focused?

You never have to be reminded from the outside to do the things that you value the most. Look at the activities, relationships, and goals for which you are disciplined, reliable, and focused – the things that nobody has to get you up to do. In which three activities and areas are you most reliable disciplined and focused?

_____

_____

_____

7. What do you think about the most?

What are your most common thoughts about how you want your life to be? What are your three most dominant thoughts?

_____

_____

_____

8. What is your internal dialogue?

What do you keep talking to yourself about the most? What are the three things that you have internal dialogues about?

_____

_____

_____

9. What do you talk about in social settings?

What are the three things or topics that you enjoy speaking about in social settings?

_____

_____

_____

10. What inspires you?

What are the three things or people that inspire you the most?

_____

_____

_____

11. What are the most consistent long-term goals that you set?

What are the three long-term goals that you have thought about the most over the years?

_____

_____

_____

12. What do you love to learn and read about most?

What are the three most common topics you love learning or reading about?

_____

_____

_____

What are your Top 4 VALUES?

The answers above should give you a good primary indicator of what your highest values are. Identify the four values that repeat most often:

1. _____

2. _____

3. _____

4. _____

EXERCISE #8 – LINK YOUR HIGHEST VALUES TO MONEY

Write down 5 reasons each on why earning $20,000 a month (or whatever your financial goal is) helps you meet each of these values. (i.e. five reasons why making $20,000 a month helps your children, five reasons why it's good for your health, your spirituality, etc.)

1. _____

2. _____

3. _____

4. _____

Is Wealth and Success HIGH On Your Hierarchy of Values?

In life, you get what is *most* important to you (what you value the most). The values that are highest on your "Hierarchy of Values" you will endure pain and pleasure to get them into your life. Some examples of values include:

- ❑ The safety and wellbeing of your children
- ❑ Watching television
- ❑ Financial Security
- ❑ Spending time with your friends
- ❑ Looking beautiful
- ❑ Being in a Relationship
- ❑ Being healthy
- ❑ Travelling
- ❑ Your career
- ❑ Getting praise from your boss
- ❑ Making a difference in your community
- ❑ Fitness; Playing sports
- ❑ Money
- ❑ Thrill-seeking

Your hierarchy of values dictates your financial destiny. Why? Because it determines how you will spend your money when it comes in. Will you spend it on eating out, a new car, fancy clothes, an exotic holiday... or will you increase your savings and invest in your business?

If achieving wealth and financial freedom is not in your "Top 4", chances are you are not going to do what it takes to become financially free. Whatever is low on your Hierarchy of Values will experience disorder and chaos. You won't be particularly inspired to make a change or follow through.

This is why the first secret in transforming your relationship to money and your financial results is **you must appreciate money more.** In other words, you must get "wealth" and "success" to rise up higher on your hierarchy of values (more on this in Chapter 2).

* * * * * * * * *

Listen To Your Heart And Live Authentically

We become fulfilled by living an *authentic* life. This means being true to ourselves by discovering our higher purpose and making a difference in people's lives.

Being on your purpose makes you feel fulfilled and happy. Having a purpose gives you focus, energy, and the power to break through your fears. Negative occurrences, setbacks, criticisms, etc. mean little to you because your *purpose* is unchanging, your determination unwavering. It doesn't matter what obstacles are encountered, you overcome them with ease when you are *on your purpose.*

Knowing Yourself Is The Most Stabilizing Thing You Can Do

"When people are true to themselves, when they are true to their values... they are inspired and they are inspiring. Nobody has to get them up and 'discipline' them to do what they need to do... Nobody has to motivate you to do what is highest on your hierarchy of values...The lower something is on your value list, the more you will require outside motivation to get you to do it."

[...] "If you have a hierarchy of values, and you meet somebody else that has a different hierarchy of values, and you put them on a pedestal, and perceive them as authority, you will inject their value system into your own, have an internal conflict, dilemma, trying to live your own value system AND theirs, and you will require outside motivation to live theirs, and have inside inspiration to live yours. And the conflict between them will create chaos. So, knowing yourself is the most stabilizing thing you can do."

Dr. John Demartini

When you wake up every morning excited about your career, and look forward to starting your day, then you will be happier, more positive, healthier, less stressed, and you will feel secure.

You feel happy when you listen to your heart and you live in accordance to your true values. That's when you are being *authentic*. It also boosts your self-esteem no end. Self-esteem means having *esteem for oneself*. You build it by doing what's hard, pushing through obstacles, challenges, and your comfort zone to create the life that inspires you. No progress means no growth, and that is death to your spirit.

In your heart you *know* what you would love to do. The truth is that *you can do* it, because you are a powerful CREATOR, with infinitely more power than you give yourself credit for. Follow your heart and you will be happy. Don't follow it and you are setting yourself up for a life of frustration and regret.

It is better to have the whole world against you than your own soul.

The cost of not following your heart, is spending the rest of your life wishing you had.

"Your soul doesn't care what you do for a living – and when your life is over, neither will you. Your soul cares only about what you are being while you are doing whatever you are doing. [...] Go ahead and do what you really love to do! Do nothing else! You have so little time! How can you think of wasting a moment doing something for a living you don't like to do? What kind of living is that? That is not a living, that is a dying!"

Neale Donald Walsch, *Conversations With God*

* * * * * * * *

41

Summary – Chapter 1

- ❑ Clarity is power.

- ❑ You get your life to take off by first becoming *very clear* about who you are and what you really want.

- ❑ The clearer you are on what you want, the faster your goals manifest.

- ❑ If you get absolutely crystal clear on exactly what you want to create in your life, and you can't see anything *but* that in your mind's eye, it is almost impossible for you not to get it.

- ❑ The people at the TOP of life spend hours planning and visualizing their life, and the people at the bottom do it the least.

- ❑ In life, you get what is highest on your Hierarchy of Values.

- ❑ Nobody has to motivate you to do what is highest on your Hierarchy of Values

- ❑ Things that are high on your Hierarchy of Values, you are willing to endure both pain and pleasure to get. People that only seek pleasure will never achieve great success or rise to a position of leadership.

- ❑ To attract more money in your life you need to *appreciate* money.

- ❑ You *appreciate* money by raising it higher on your Hierarchy of Values.

- ❑ One way of doing this is by linking "money and success" to your highest values.

- ❑ Knowing yourself is the most stabilizing thing you can do.

- ❑ We become fulfilled by living an authentic life. This means being true to ourselves by discovering our higher purpose and making a difference in people's lives.

- ❑ Don't chase after money. Instead, be on a mission and ADD MASSIVE VALUE.

- ❑ A MISSION is the best way to meet the most amount of your values while adding the most amount of value to others.

❑ You are a powerful CREATOR.

❑ It is better to have the whole world against you than your own soul.

CHAPTER 2

Develop Your Millionaire Mind

As I completed the first section of exercises given to me by Balthazar, I began feeling very excited. I could see my life ahead of me very clearly. My dreams had laid on a shelf of my mind for many years, moribund, gathering dust, it seemed, but suddenly they were coming back to life, in vivid colour.

Somewhere deep inside of me I started feeling like my time in this dilapidated rat-infested building was coming to an end. I could see a new life for myself, just over the horizon.

I delved back into the book and continued on with the exercises, while biting into an apple. That would be my only meal that day.

* * * * * * * *

Most people believe that by simply changing their **actions**, their life will get better. The truth is that they need to go 'upstream', if they truly want to change their life: they need to first identify and change their subconscious thoughts and beliefs.

Only then will their choices, decisions, and actions—stemming from their subconscious beliefs—start producing different results. In fact, this will happen automatically.

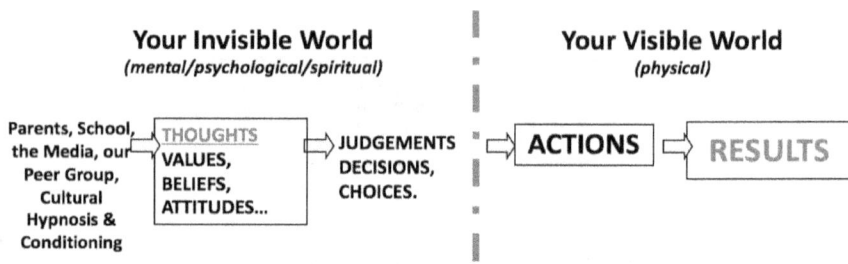

Your Invisible World
(mental/psychological/spiritual)

Your Visible World
(physical)

Parents, School, the Media, our Peer Group, Cultural Hypnosis & Conditioning → THOUGHTS VALUES, BELIEFS, ATTITUDES... → JUDGEMENTS DECISIONS, CHOICES. → **ACTIONS** → RESULTS

The "ITJAR" Model: your Identity/Thoughts/Values/Beliefs (your psychology) determines your Judgement, Choices and Decisions, cascading into your Actions and RESULTS.

People change jobs, cities, relationships, houses, cars, diets, business opportunities… and are surprised at how they experience *yet again* the exact same problems, the same aggravations, the same arguments, the same weight gain, the same lowly pay.

It is because they changed their actions, but not their beliefs. You see, to change your life you need to work on the root of the problem. Money is the "fruit" of consistently excellent subconscious beliefs about money, success, and about yourself.

Your thoughts and beliefs (your "invisible" world) create your *visible* world. This is **the key insight** that would change everything in my life… (more on that later).

As author Stewart Swerdlow explains:

"Physical reality is the screen or the mirror that allows us to see/reflect our own thinking. When you take responsibility for your thinking, your life gets much better. When you don't take responsibility for your thinking… it gets worse. No one is a victim. No one is being punished. Everyone is creating their own life. WE are creating it.

If you don't like the movie that is playing… you've got to

<u>change the FILM</u> being projected onto the screen of your life. You've got to *think differently* so that there's a different movie playing. Your thought is the film. The brain is the projector. Physical reality is the screen."

For example, if you believe that "making money is hard", that is exactly what you will perceive around you and what you will experience in your own life. You will naturally take actions that are aligned with the belief that "making money is hard" and will struggle to make ends meet. To change that 'reality', you need change *your beliefs*.

Why not adopt this new belief: **Making money is fun and easy!**

Earl Nightingale, author of *The Strangest Secret,* stated in 1957: "We live in a world of cause and effect. THOUGHTS are causes, and your present conditions are the EFFECT. We must control our thoughts in order to control our lives." Brian Tracy wrote: "Your outer world is a reflection of your inner world, and it corresponds to your dominant patterns of thinking. **You become what you think about most of the time.** Change your thinking, and you will change your life."

Could the beliefs of poor and middle-class people lead them to experiencing lack or struggle?

Here are some of the negative beliefs about money that my friend Henry—a security guard colleague of mine—had:

❏ "Money doesn't buy you happiness."
❏ "Money can't buy you love."
❏ "It is not fair that some people have more than others."
❏ "I can't make a lot of money... it is hard to make money."
❏ "People fight over money, so it is better to not have any."
❏ "If I make a lot of money I'll get sucked in. What about my spiritual side?"
❏ "Money doesn't grow on trees (it's hard to make money)"
❏ "To get rich you have to take it from someone else. You'll have more and they'll have less. It's not fair..."

- ❑ "To make money you have to take advantage of other people, and I would never…"
- ❑ "There isn't enough." (lack consciousness)
- ❑ "If I make more money than my friends they won't like me anymore."
- ❑ "I'm not good enough. I don't deserve more money and happiness."
- ❑ "What if I make a lot of money and lose it all? Then I'm really a failure!"
- ❑ "I am afraid of failure. What if I fail? What will people think of me?"
- ❑ "I am afraid of rejection. What if people don't like my product?"
- ❑ "Rich people are greedy, exploitative, selfish. But I am a good person."
- ❑ "Money is the root of all evil."
- ❑ "In order to make more money I'll have to work harder, I won't have time to enjoy it, so why even try?"
- ❑ "To make money you need to be really smart, and I'm not smart enough…"
- ❑ "If I make more money I'll never know if people like me for me or my money."

Now, my friend George who was a waiter at a Greek restaurant in London at the time had an altogether different mindset regarding money:

- ❑ "Making money is easy! Making money is fun!"
- ❑ "Making a lot of money is extremely important!"
- ❑ "Money is nothing but the measure of the value I create for other people!"
- ❑ "Money is nothing but the manifestation of my resourcefulness!"
- ❑ "I find out what problems people have and I help them by providing solutions!"

❑ "I get paid in direct proportion to the amount of value I deliver according to the marketplace!"

❑ "There are millions of people out there who need what I have and what I know!"

❑ "All skills are learnable! If I don't know how to, I find someone who does!"

❑ "I create my life! I can create anything I want with the power of my creative mind!"

❑ "I hate being broke! Being broke means I am being selfish with my gifts, intellect, ability, and love. Being broke means I am too afraid to stand on my own two feet, and instead must rely on getting a salary from someone. Being broke means I am not adding huge amounts of value to people!"

❑ "I am worth it! I **deserve** wealth and abundance!"

❑ "I can make a lot of money doing what I love!"

❑ "It is thanks to the efforts of entrepreneurs that the economy grows. By organizing the efforts of people, capital, creativity, time... Entrepreneurs create more value.... Raising *everyone's* wealth and standard of living."

❑ "Failure just makes me learn how to succeed better & faster! The only failure is to not try!"

❑ "There are 36 million millionaires globally... there are $241 trillion in global wealth... there is money everywhere!" (abundance consciousness)

❑ "I don't care about rejection... I just need one person to say 'yes' to me and I'm in business!"

❑ "I love making money! I can help and support my family and children better!"

❑ "I love making money! I can afford to take better care of my health and fitness!"

❑ "I love making money! I love being rich! I get help a lot of people, I get to create a lot of jobs, and I get to enjoy the best that life has to offer!"

That's a pretty huge difference in points of view, wouldn't you agree? Now, while both Henry and George started out earning minimum wage and had the same level of education, something interesting happened. George ended up saving some money and getting into a real estate development business. He became a multi-millionaire by age 34. Henry, on the other hand, remains a security guard to this day. He is morbidly obese, single, and extremely unhappy.

What separated them at the start?

In one word: their <u>mindset</u>.

According to the book handed to me by Balthazar, the first thing that differentiates successful people from the rest was the idea of "creating value."

* * * * * * * * *

Millionaire Mindset Secret #1:
The Wealthy Focus On Creating VALUE

If you want to create wealth in your life, you need to produce and deliver *more value*.

You see, money is just a means of exchange, between one person's value for another. It has no moral value, it's neither right or wrong, good or bad, positive or negative.

People used to barter goods. They would exchange five chickens for twelve bales of hay, for example. Money was created as a token that *represents* real-world value (such as food, goods, or work-hours), to facilitate the *exchange* of value between people (also known as 'commerce').

The more 'chickens' and 'bales of hay' you produce, the more of these 'tokens' flow to you. This is why traditionally, the person with the most LAND was the richest person in that area...

Rich and successful people have a fundamentally different view of money than poor or middle-class people. One of the biggest "a-ha" moments of my life came when I read the following sentence in Balthazar's book:

"Money Is Nothing But The Measure Of The Value You Create For Other People!"

He had mentioned it during our meeting, but I had been too emotional at the time for it to really "land." The money in your bank account is simply a <u>representation</u> of how much value you consistently provide to people. This was quite a departure from what I had been told my whole life. It changed my entire perspective on wealth and success.

You see, my father's beliefs were more of the "rich-people-have-too-much-money-and-it's-unfair" variety. His beliefs included: "Rich people are greedy, evil, exploitative! We are good people... and that's why we have no money..." and "The only way to get rich... is to bribe the Greek government!"

But now I could realistically see a path to achieving great wealth. As long as I used my creativity to figure out how to **add value** to people, and as long as I kept learning about wealth creation, success, business-building, and investing... I was bound to become successful.
This notion of "adding value" kept coming up as I studied successful people and their "success principles." The well-known sales trainer and personal development author Zig Ziglar wrote:

"You can get everything in life you want if you just help enough other people get what they want."

Earl Nightingale stated:

"You become rich by enriching others!"

Brian Tracy added:

"The Law of Income states that **you get paid in direct proportion to the amount of value you deliver** according to the marketplace!"

The lesson here for entrepreneurs is: don't chase after the money. Instead, focus on how many customers you want to serve and add value to them—the bigger the problem you solve for them, the more money they'll pay you. Building a business, after all, boils down to two simple things: customer acquisition (marketing and sales) and customer nurturing (staying in touch with your customers and offering them further products and services after the initial sale).

In this model of the world, you create win-win situations. The more value you provide, the happier your clients are and the wealthier you become.

I quickly realized that I would have to master the topic of "marketing" if I was to have a successful business... Dan Kennedy, the author of "63 Killer Marketing Strategies", states in his book:

> "No matter what business you are in… you are in the marketing business! Marketing is about sharing your gift. And you become wealthy adding value to large numbers of people. **But how can you add value to people if you don't know how to reach them?**
>
> Waiting around to be discovered, to be recognized, to be noticed, to be appointed, to be promoted guarantees one thing and one thing only: old age. Focusing on doing whatever it is that you do better than anybody else and trusting that alone is enough guarantees one thing and one thing only: a long life of labor in oblivion."

How Do You Create More Value?

If adding more value is the key to creating great wealth, how do you do so? How do you enrich others? How do you help them get what they want?

It starts by asking yourself a different set of questions. A better *quality* of questions can unlock your creativity and tap into your abundant capacities for resourcefulness.

Instead of asking "How can I make more money?" ask yourself:

- ❏ Quality Question #1: What problems do people have?

- ❏ Quality Question #2: What do people WANT?

- ❏ Quality Question #3: What Are people BUYING?

- ❏ Quality Question #4: How Can I Add More VALUE? How Can I Add 100 Times More Value?

- ❏ Quality Question #5: What Solutions Can I Provide To People's Problems?

- ❏ Quality Question #6: Where Can I SOURCE Great Products or Solutions For People?

- ❏ Quality Question #7: How Can I Get Paid To Do What I Love?

- ❏ Quality Question #8: What are 30 Ways HOW I can raise $50,000 to launch my business?

You see, if you are asking yourself "How can I make more money", the focus is on *you*. It is a selfish quest. No one will give you money just because *you* want money. They'll give you money in exchange for goods or services you'll provide them.

So, by asking yourself a quality question such as "What problems do people have?" or "What solutions do people need?", you are on your way to winning the game of money. You are already *thinking like a millionaire,* rather than thinking like most people out there, who are too lazy, greedy, or self-centered to do what it really takes to become wealthy.

Another key insight is this: to deliver more value, sell products rather than selling your time. There are no limits to how many products you can create or sell, therefore your earning potential becomes uncapped (unlimited). Furthermore, every product can become a new income stream, and you get to access a global market.

Most people are trained from a young age to sell their *time*. But they only have so much time to sell—which limits their wealth potential dramatically—and furthermore, since everyone else is selling their time too, there are millions of workers out there competing for the same jobs. Their qualifications are exactly the same, so this depresses the price they can sell their time for. Their time and skills have become commoditized.

In any case, being an employee is *not* the best way to produce huge amounts of value. Instead of selling your time, focus on building a business, creating systems, and selling products.

Here are some tips on how you can start creating and delivering more value:

- ❑ Learn more. Increase the value of *you* (your know-how and skills).

- ❑ Sell products; by selling products, you are no longer exchanging time for money. Your earning potential becomes uncapped.

- ❑ Get agents, joint venture partners, sales people and affiliates to sell your products for a commission. You are giving them a way for *them* to earn money. You are creating value for them *and* for the end user.

- ❑ Leverage the Internet, Technology, Systems, Affiliates, Advertising, Social Media, Search Engines, Newsletters, Capital, Amazon, iTunes, eBay, Networks, Employees, Outsourcers, etc. to sell more products to more people.

- ❑ Sell to a global market. Nowadays, you can sell through Facebook, YouTube, Clickbank, Google, Amazon, iTunes, eBay, Audible, and thousands of other websites to people *all over the world!* The power at your fingertips is huge.

- ❑ Build a TEAM so that they deliver your products and services to more people.

- ❑ License products, software, content, etc. to add to your offer, to increase its overall value.

- ❑ Brainstorm 100 Ways How You Can Add Value. Brainstorm 30 "irresistible offers".

❑ Learn to sell – nothing happens until a sale is made. You can't deliver mass amounts of value if you don't know how to *sell* that value.

If someone feels that they are not making enough money, chances are they are either not producing enough value, or they are not using enough leverage.

THE LAW OF PROSPERITY: Produce more than you consume.

"Our entire financial system is based on debt and consumption. You always hear, for example, how the American consumer drives the US economy. You don't ever hear anyone say that the American manufacturer... or the American capitalist... drives the US economy. It's all about consumption, not production. This constitutes a willful violation of the Universal Law of Prosperity."

Simon Black, founder of SovereignMan.com

Become a Producer

We have been conditioned from birth to be good "Consumers", but to consume means to burn up or destroy. Instead, become a great producer. Produce VALUE, produce SOLUTIONS, produce FOOD, produce PRODUCTS, produce SERVICES that people need.

A common limiting belief that people have is that "*it takes money to make money*". Millionaires know better. Money is simply a resource—one that is abundantly available, at that. To make money doesn't require money, it requires *resourcefulness*. If you train your mind to be "resourceful", you will find the money or you will find the way to start your business.

Here are some examples of how you can start a business with no money down, as I have, by being resourceful:

❑ I launched my ebook selling business in 2004, just 28 days after completing Balthazar's exercises. I had no money to invest, so I told my web designer *"I'll pay you after I start making money from this*

55

site...". And I did. He set up the website for me, and it started generating $10,000 a month in passive income within a month.

❏ Create a product by interviewing experts: in 2010 I interviewed 12 YouTube marketing experts, I created a course with this content (videos, MP3s, and a PDF) and charged $2,500 for it. Within two months I made 100 sales and $250,000 in sales. In 2011 I interviewed ten Facebook marketing experts and created a course on this topic. I did a product launch on Clickbank and got 400 affiliates to promote it. We did $400,000 in sales in 30 days.

❏ Create a product by licensing content: my client Tom H. licensed a 'Facebook friend adder' software, added some valuable content to it, and created a webinar presentation to sell it. Thanks to joint venture webinars, he did a massive $2.5 million in sales in just four months.

❏ Pick up the phone and sell something! for example, find outsourcers in a specific area (e.g. SEO, voice over actors, graphic designers, etc.), create an agency, and sell their services at a premium.

❏ Joint Venture: bring something to the table—a product, or marketing know-how—and joint venture with an expert that has a following. Alternatively: help the expert sell his products through Facebook, Amazon, or through webinars.

❏ Also: you can start a business part-time; or buy a business with no money down, when a business owner wants to get out of their own business; or become a business partner; partner with someone who has the capital, the product, the marketing know-how, or the contacts needed for the business to be successful (you need to bring something to the table as well, even if it's only your time).

❏ Write a business plan and raise funds. In 2006 I needed to raise £40,000 to put on a big event in London, so I wrote a one-page business proposal and sent it to twenty entrepreneurs I knew in the UK. Instead of thinking to myself "I can't afford it..." I asked myself a better question: HOW can I afford it? I managed to secure the funds. Two months later our event generated £400,000 and I paid back the investor… ahead of time!

So you see. money is nothing but the manifestation of *your resourcefulness*—and what is resourcefulness? It is a MINDSET!

Millionaire Mindset Secret #2:
The Wealthy Are Persistent And Determined

Typically, self-made millionaires display a mindset of **persistence**, **desire**, and **commitment** that are uncommon in the general population.

So many people nowadays seem to be lazy and greedy—they want all the rewards, but none of the work. They want free money from the state (welfare), to get on a reality TV show and be "famous", or to win the lottery. Rich people think differently.

For starters, they have a burning desire to achieve.

It's never a question of *can* you do it—others have done it, therefore *so can you*—but rather *will* you do it. It comes down to your motivation and desire. Many people find that they start earning more when they take on a mortgage. If someone took your children and wife and told you "you will never see your wife or children again unless you earn $100,000 in the next month…" you would get out of your comfort zone, become resourceful, come up with new ideas, and you would do whatever it takes to earn that money.

You think you can't raise one million pounds? What if I told you there was a ten-million-dollar mansion available for just $1m *today*. Would you figure out how to raise the funds? It's never about a lack of money. It's a question of *lack of motivation*. What *you* need to do is figure out a goal or a cause that would truly motivate you to go beyond yourself—something that is congruent with your values and that inspires you on a *soul* level.

They are determined and committed.

Wealth flows to the person who has a high tolerance for uncertainty or disappointment. Handle disappointment well, and you will make more attempts to achieve your goals.

57

Keep going *until* you succeed. Show tenacity, determination, commitment. Ask 20 investors for the seed capital you need. 19 rejections just takes you closer to your goal! You only need one person to say 'YES!'

Millionaire Mindset Secret #3:
The Wealthy BELIEVE In Themselves

Believe in yourself and develop an attitude of positive optimism. You you can achieve anything you set your mind to! If others have done it, so can you. Be confident and self-assured. You are following your dreams. It does not matter one iota what other people think of you.

Loving yourself is the vital first step towards enjoying an abundant and impactful life. A lot of people suffer from **low self-worth issues**, often stemming from childhood, which can lead to self-sabotage, self-sacrifice, and subconscious feelings of "being not good enough".

Do you believe you must struggle? Do you believe you don't deserve success and wealth? Financial lack is a way of affirming these negative mind-patterns. Lack can be the result of feelings of guilt or a belief that "I don't deserve good things." I had to do a lot of work on myself, with daily affirmations and release work (the 'Golden Altar' and 'Child Within' exercises) to let go of such issues and learn to love myself…

It is a fallacy to believe that wealth and prosperity will manifest themselves in your life before you deal with those issues, or that success will magically make those issues go away. That is not how things work. You don't become successful *when* you get a lot of money… That would be putting the horse before the cart. You get attract prosperity *when* you become a successful person! In other words, sort out your mindset first, and abundance will follow.

It is important to realize that we live in a world of massive abundance. There are TRILLIONS of dollars (pounds, euros…) circulating around us at all times… They are available to you too… The Universe is waiting for you to declare… "I AM WORTH IT!"

It is crucial that you BELIEVE in yourself. You've got to recognize and realize the value you have within yourself before others can see it as well.

Feel like you DESERVE IT, without guilt, fear of jealousy, or resentment. KNOW that you deserve it, no matter what anyone else says. A great affirmation for this is: "I now attract, receive, and ACCEPT all the abundance and prosperity of the Universe."

If you hold on to feelings of **guilt**, you are carrying baggage around. Your feelings of worth and your willingness to receive abundance are interfered with. Eliminate those feelings of guilt and raise your self-worth.

Whenever you receive an inheritance or an unexpected large sum of money, write down what you did to deserve it. Because if you don't feel like you deserve it, you will probably find a way—subconsciously—to squander that money.

Let go and forgive the past. It will open up your finances. Let go of the negative space-holders in your life so the positive ones have room to manifest. For example, as a man, if you make your father wrong, you're going to have problems in your career. If you make your mother wrong, you're going to have problems in your relationships. (For women, it is inversed: make your mother wrong and you'll have problems in your career; make your father wrong, and you'll have problems in your relationships).

Millionaire Mindset Secret #4:
The Wealthy Think BIG.

Because the wealthy believe in themselves, this is reflected in the size of their ambition and goals. The size of your thinking determines the size of your results.

Ultimately, you are only limited by the size of your ambition and the scope of your creativity. It takes the same amount of energy to think BIG than to think small. Use your imagination… and raise your standards!

Hang out with successful people who think BIG, who have high standards for themselves, and who have a big vision for their lives. You are more likely to have million-dollar ideas when you hang out with millionaires. It's a resonation game. *You become who you spend time with.*

Millionaire Mindset Secret #5:
The Wealthy Are GRATEFUL

Wealth and abundance exist at a frequency of GRATITUDE. To *attract* wealth into your life, you must align yourself with the vibrational frequency of people who are abundant. You do so by cultivating an attitude of *gratitude*. There is no more powerful statement to the Universe, or more powerful wealth-attraction attitude than to feel grateful for all it has already provided for you.

By adopting an attitude of gratitude no matter what happens, you are thanking the universe for the abundance in your life, and showing the Universe that you deserve more of the 'good stuff' in your life. To those who are GRATEFUL, the Universe will give MORE!

In any case, feelings of gratitude improve the quality of your life. Are you someone that feels angry all the time? Well, your quality of life sucks. Are you a minimum-wage worker that is grateful and appreciates every moment in their life? You have riches beyond compare.

Millionaire Mindset Secret #6:
The Wealthy Have A Cause That Is Bigger Than Themselves

If you have no money whatsoever, and you're starving, you would be very grateful to receive $1,000, right? You would do quite a lot to get that $1,000, right? But if you have $100,000 or $1,000,000 in the bank and you are financially secure, that same $1,000 doesn't seem particularly motivating, now does it?

That is one of the great paradoxes of wealth building: the more money you have the less money motivates you. Every time you earn another $1,000, you have a diminishing motivation to earn *another* $1,000. Building wealth, ironically, increases inertia towards building wealth.

A lot of successful people plateau and stagnate the second they have accumulated a certain amount of money. They stop working as hard, or saving money as much, or being focused, because it's not valuable to them...

That's why you have to have a cause that is bigger than you, so that you keep growing.

The author Anthony Robbins tells the story of how in the early 1990s he kept earning $1m a year for a number of years. He couldn't break through that ceiling. The following year he set as a goal to feed all the homeless people of San Diego. Because of his new goal, he made $3m that year.

This example resonates with me because for a number of years I couldn't break through the 7-figure mark myself. At $1m a year in revenue, I felt like all my needs were met. I didn't feel particularly motivated to push *beyond* that point. Until, that is, I decided to devote my life to a greater cause. A bigger vision.

You will only do so much for yourself. You will do way more if it is to help people you care about.

Why are you building wealth? Is it just for your retirement, or for your own comfort? That is a small cause. If you are building wealth for a noble cause on the other hand...

Millionaire Mindset Secret #7:
The Wealthy Appreciate Money

One of the biggest keys in developing a millionaire mind is that **you must appreciate money.** If you are in a relationship with a person that you don't appreciate or value, does the relationship tend to grow and prosper, or does it tend to decay and die? The very word 'appreciation' means *'to grow in value'*.

Appreciate that money is extremely important in your life. Appreciate and *value* having money in your life. Appreciate the opportunities that it brings.

When you appreciate money, more is given to you. Interestingly, people who appreciate money tend to put their money in things that APPRECIATE in value, while those who do not tend to put their money in things that depreciate in value!

I often hear people say *"money is not important to me... I don't care about money"* or *"I'm not in it for the money"*... and yet they work 45 years of their life in jobs that they hate. Why? *For the money!* That seems a bit hypocritical, wouldn't you agree? With those words they are actively *devaluing* money and pushing it out of their life.

Conversely, appreciating money means putting it higher on your value list—this shift in your values will bring a dramatic shift in your financial DESTINY!

The exercise below will help you exponentially expand your appreciation of money. You will write down 200 reasons why money is *good* in your life. You see... to overcome the brain's limiting beliefs about money, we need to *convince it* and overload it with "positive associations" to money.

When I completed this exercise myself, after attending that seminar, I realized that earning £2,000 a month—my big goal at the time—meant that I could help my sisters... I could help my mother... I could move into an apartment... I could buy food... Each reason was another positive association to money; another neural pathway reinforcing the belief that money is *good*.

This exercise in one fell swoop had eliminated dozens of my limiting beliefs. Inner conflicts about money disappeared. Making money shot up in my Hierarchy of Values. I began to value money much more, thus aligning my values with those of wealthy people.

Now it's your turn!

EXERCISE #9 – THE '200 REASONS WHY' EXERCISE

Our neurology is designed to keep us moving towards pleasure and away from pain. When you are a child and you touch a hot stove, ouch! Your brain has just created a strong 'neuro-association' that 'hot stove = pain'. A neural pathway has been traced in your brain, that links 'stove' with 'pain'. Later in life, when you grow up, you might get your heart broken by your girlfriend leaving you. The neuro-association created, depending on your decision in that moment, could be that 'relationships = pain'.

A teacher tells you off and ridicules you in front of the class because of your wrong spelling. You could interpret that event as 'I am = stupid'. You could also interpret it as 'That teacher = mean', or 'All teachers are mean', or 'It doesn't matter because I am really good at maths', or 'I'll get really good at spelling so that I never experience this pain again'.

When you ask your brain to come up with 200 reasons why you must have something, you are forcing it to create 200 'neuro-associations' (neural pathway linkages) between the concept of what you want (e.g. to earn $10,000 a month, to be in a loving relationship, or to get that dream job) and the part of your brain where the concept of pleasure resides.

When I wrote down 200 reasons why I must make £2,000 a month, I forced my brain to overload itself with 200 neuro-associations that said 'money = good' and 'money = pleasure'! Your brain cannot hold onto its fabricated belief system that 'money is bad' when it itself had to come up with 200 reasons why the opposite is true.

Your brain will try to sabotage you and keep you in your comfort zone every step of the way. "You wrote down 10 reasons already? Great! Well done. Now STOP this exercise and go reward yourself with some pizza and ice cream…"

Make sure you **push through these mental barriers until you get all the way to 200.** There is real transformation to be achieved when you do so.

These questions below will help you come up with more **reasons why**:

- ❑ What will it COST YOU if you don't achieve financial freedom? What would you miss out on? What would you stress about? How would this affect your relationship?
- ❑ What PAIN will you or your children be able to avoid by becoming wealthy?
- ❑ What things will you be able to buy? What debts will you pay off?
- ❑ What seminars or courses will you be able to attend, to help you grow and evolve?
- ❑ How will you be able to help your family, friends, and loved ones?
- ❑ How will you be able to have more fun with your friends?
- ❑ How will you be able to quit your job and start the career you've always wanted?
- ❑ What house will you be able to move to? Where will you live?
- ❑ What countries will you be able to travel to?
- ❑ What will you be able to create?
- ❑ What hobbies will you be able to indulge? Painting? Music?
- ❑ What kind of life will you be able to provide your children?
- ❑ How will this eliminate the stress, aggravation & fear in your life?
- ❑ What charities or causes will you be able to contribute to?

Write down 200 reasons why you <u>MUST</u> make _____ a month:

1) _____

2) _____

3) _____

4) _____

5) _____

6) _____

7) _____

8) _____

9) _____

10) _____

11) _____

12) _____

13) _____

14) _____

15) _____

16) _____

17) _____

18) _____

19) _____

20) _____

21) _____

22) _____

23) _____

24) _____

25) _____

26) _____

27) _____

28) _____

29) _____

30) _____

31) _____

32) _____

33) _____

34) _____

35) _____

36) _____

37) _____

38) _____

39) _____

40) _____

41) _____

42) _____

43) _____

44) _____

45) _____

46) _____

47) _____

48) _____

49) _____

50) _____

51) _____

52) _____

53) _____

54) _____

55) _____

56) _____

57) _____

57) _____

58) _____

59) _____

60) _____

61) _____

62) _____

63) _____

64) _____

65) _____

66) _____

67) _____

68) _____

69) _____

70) _____

71) _____

72) _____

73) _____

74) _____

75) _____

76) _____

77) _____

78) _____

79) _____

80) _____

81) _____

82) _____

83) _____

84) _____

85) _____

86) _____

87) _____

88) _____

89) _____

90) _____

91) _____

92) _____

93) _____

94) _____

95) _____

96) _____

97) _____

98) _____

99) _____

100) _____

101) _____

102) _____

103) _____

104) _____

105) _____

106) _____

107) _____

108) _____

109) _____

110) _____

111) _____

112) _____

113) _____

114) _____

115) _____

116) _____

117) _____

118) _____

119) _____

120) _____

121) _____

122) _____

123) _____

124) _____

125) _____

126) _____

127) _____

128) _____

129) _____

130) _____

131) _____

132) _____

133) _____

134) _____

135) _____

136) _____

137) _____

138) _____

139) _____

140) _____

141) _____

142) _____

143) _____

144) _____

145) _____

146) _____

147) _____

148) _____

149) _____

150) _____

151) _____

152) _____

153) _____

154) _____

155) _____

156) _____

157) _____

157) _____

158) _____

159) _____

160) _____

161) _____

162) _____

163) _____

164) _____

165) _____

166) _____

167) _____

168) _____

169) _____

170) _____

171) _____

172) _____

173) _____

174) _____

175) _____

176) _____

177) _____

178) _____

179) _____

180) _____

181) _____

182) _____

183) _____

184) _____

185) _____

186) _____

187) _____

188) _____

189) _____

190) _____

191) _____

192) _____

193) _____

194) _____

195) _____

196) _____

197) _____

198) _____

199) _____

200) _____

Note: You can apply this exercise to other goals, such as getting into a relationship, losing weight, increasing your sales, buying your first house, regaining your health… It is very powerful.

EXERCISE #10 – NOTICE THE ABUNDANCE

Millionaires and wealthy people in general tend to focus on abundance, rather than live from a place of lack and scarcity.

The Law of Attraction states that fear attracts like energy and **what you focus on expands**. Focus on scarcity and… you only attract more scarcity in your life. Conversely, if you focus on everything you have, everything you are grateful for, and on all the abundance available around you… then you will move towards experiencing abundance in your own life.

See the abundance of resources, love, relationships, wealth, opportunities… all around you. An endless supply! Remind yourself that there is more than enough. Celebrate other people's successes.

Focus on adding value, rather than on 'taking' from others. Focus on becoming resourceful and coming up with *solutions*, rather than focus on your 'problems'.

There are 241 TRILLION DOLLARS in circulation currently across the global economy. There is money on every street, in every house, in every car, in every town, in every city, in every country, on every continent… there is PLENTY of money around!

Look at all the incredible infrastructure that has been built around you! the buildings, the roads, the airports, the planes, the restaurants, the sewage systems, the water pipes, the electricity grid… hundreds of trillions of dollars! YOU didn't need to pay for *any* of that!

Exercise: List all the abundance, wealth, and assets you possess (material and immaterial). List where you already have that value that you are seeking (e.g. $1m, $5m, or $20m), perhaps in your skills, knowledge, contacts, business ideas, unfinished products or projects...

_____

_____

_____

_____

_____

_____

_____

_____

_____

_____

_____

_____

_____

_____

_____

_____

_____

_____

_____

73

_____

_____

_____

_____

_____

_____

List 10 Ways how people are making a FORTUNE right now.

(e.g. technology breakthroughs, social media websites, robotics, artificial intelligence, 3D printing, software, 'apps', publishing, producing movies, new trends in society, etc.)

1) _____

2) _____

3) _____

4) _____

5) _____

6) _____

7) _____

8) _____

9) _____

10) _____

EXERCISE #11 – BE RESOURCEFUL!

How can you get paid to do what you love?

_____

_____

_____

_____

_____

_____

_____

_____

_____

_____

_____

_____

_____

_____

_____

_____

_____

_____

How can you create or deliver more value?

_____

_____

_____

_____

_____

_____

_____

_____

_____

_____

_____

_____

_____

_____

Watch Your FREE Video Training

"The 10 Secrets To Developing an 'Abundance' Mindset"

www.LifeCanBeAwesome.com

EXERCISE #12 – THE "100 WAYS HOW" EXERCISE

People severely underestimate what their mind is capable of achieving for them, if they would just use it! Ask your mind a better question, and it will bring you better answers.

By asking my mind to come up with 100 ways how I could earn £2,000 a month—I completed this exercise the day after meeting with Balthazar—it obliged. Initially I only knew of three ways: send out a CV and pray for a job, buying and selling real estate in London, and... Herbalife (multi-level marketing). That was it. That was the extent of my 'wealth creation' knowledge.

Nonetheless, over a period of three days and after much research, I came up with a list of 100 ways. I would have never come up with that lucrative 93rd idea on the list, if I hadn't done this exercise... You see, to have a GREAT idea, you need to have MANY ideas!

28 days after completing this exercise I had my first internet business bringing in more than $300 a day in passive income. This exercise had collapsed my limiting beliefs "I don't know how to make a lot of money" and "making money is hard."

Whenever I feel stuck with a problem, by the way, I grab my journal and brainstorm 20 or so actions I can take to resolve the situation, or names of people that can help. And whenever I feel like procrastinating, I brainstorm 20 or so reasons why I must complete the task. This works!

To help you complete this exercise, think about...

- ❏ Your skillset, and ways how you can add value to people, who you can help
- ❏ Think about solutions that you can bring to the table
- ❏ Business opportunities you've heard about
- ❏ Investment opportunities
- ❏ Licensing opportunities
- ❏ Franchising opportunities

- ❑ Internet marketing opportunities
- ❑ Publishing opportunities
- ❑ Webinar opportunities
- ❑ Arbitrage opportunities
- ❑ Trading opportunities
- ❑ Joint venture opportunities
- ❑ Direct mail opportunities
- ❑ Banner advertising and pay-per-click advertising opportunities
- ❑ Social media management and traffic-generation-done-for-you opportunities
- ❑ Done-for-you services opportunities
- ❑ Blogging business opportunities
- ❑ Amazon and ecommerce opportunities
- ❑ Dropshipping opportunities
- ❑ Passive income opportunities
- ❑ Ebook selling opportunities
- ❑ Newsletter publishing opportunities
- ❑ Real estate opportunities…

There are, literally, THOUSANDS of ways of making money! Open your mind!

Brainstorm 100 ways HOW you can earn _____ a month! (fill the blank with your own financial goal, e.g. $20,000/month)

1) _____

2) _____

3) _____

4) _____

5) _____

6) _____

7) _____

8) _____

9) _____

10) _____

11) _____

12) _____

13) _____

14) _____

15) _____

16) _____

17) _____

18) _____

19) _____

20) _____

21) _____

22) _____

23) _____

24) _____

25) _____

26) _____

27) _____

28) _____

29) _____

30) _____

31) _____

32) _____

33) _____

34) _____

35) _____

36) _____

37) _____

38) _____

39) _____
40) _____
41) _____
42) _____
43) _____
44) _____
45) _____
46) _____
47) _____
48) _____
49) _____
50) _____
51) _____
52) _____
53) _____
54) _____
55) _____
56) _____
57) _____
57) _____
58) _____
59) _____
60) _____
61) _____
62) _____
63) _____
64) _____
65) _____

66) _____

67) _____

68) _____

69) _____

70) _____

71) _____

72) _____

73) _____

74) _____

75) _____

76) _____

77) _____

78) _____

79) _____

80) _____

81) _____

82) _____

83) _____

84) _____

85) _____

86) _____

87) _____

88) _____

89) _____

90) _____

91) _____

92) _____

93) _____

94) _____

95) _____

96) _____

97) _____

98) _____

99) _____

100) _____

Make sure you complete this exercise <u>all the way to 100</u>! It will activate a long dormant part of your brain, and you will begin to see solutions (and opportunities) everywhere. Your financial circumstances will improve measurably when you become a powerful solution-finding and value-adding genius.

And remember: your biggest resource is your own resourcefulness!

EXERCISE #13 – THE GRATITUDE EXERCISE

Gratitude aligns you with the frequency of prosperity, happiness, and success. Write down 20 things you are GRATEFUL for in your life:

1) _____

2) _____

3) _____

4) _____

5) _____

6) _____

7) _____

8) _____

9) _____

10) _____

11) _____

12) _____

13) _____

14) _____

15) _____

16) _____

17) _____

18) _____

19) _____

20) _____

EXERCISE #14 – THE SELF-LOVE EXERCISE

Write down 20 things you LOVE about yourself:

1) _____
2) _____
3) _____
4) _____
5) _____
6) _____
7) _____
8) _____
9) _____
10) _____
11) _____
12) _____
13) _____
14) _____
15) _____
16) _____
17) _____
18) _____
19) _____
20) _____

Write down 20 things you have achieved and/or are PROUD of:

1) _____

2) _____

3) _____

4) _____

5) _____

6) _____

7) _____

8) _____

9) _____

10) _____

11) _____

12) _____

13) _____

14) _____

15) _____

16) _____

17) _____

18) _____

19) _____

20) _____

EXERCISE #15 – LETTING GO OF GUILT

Write down 5 things you think you have messed up or 'screwed up' in your life:

_____

_____

_____

_____

_____

_____

Then, write down:

❑ How did it serve you?

_____

_____

_____

_____

_____

❑ How did it serve others? (5 things for each)

_____

_____

_____

_____

_____

_____

_____

_____

_____

_____

_____

_____

_____

_____

_____

_____

_____

Note: Upon completion of this exercise, notice how your perceptions of guilt subside.

EXERCISE #16 – THE 'CREATING THE VOID' EXERCISE

In order to **attract** more money into your life, you need to create a **void** for it to fill… Why would the Universe allow wealth into your life, if you have no *use* for it? Why would the universe give you $1,000,000 if you don't even know what to do with it?

If you want $1,000,000 or $20,000,000, write down what you will DO with that sum. How is it going to be allocated? What will you do to DESERVE $20,000,000? What SERVICE will you provide in exchange for that sum?

Describe what would you spend $250,000 on if you received this amount this year… How you would allocate these funds?

_____

_____

_____

_____

_____

_____

_____

_____

_____

_____

_____

_____

_____

_____

_____

_____

_____

_____

_____

_____

_____

What would you spend $1,000,000 on if you received this amount? How would you allocate these funds?

_____

_____

_____

_____

_____

_____

_____

_____

_____

_____

_____

_____

_____

What would you spend $20,000,000 on if you received this amount? How would you allocate these funds?

_____

_____

_____

_____

_____

_____

_____

_____

_____

_____

_____

_____

_____

_____

_____

_____

_____

_____

What would you spend $134,560,000 on if you received this amount in the next 12 months? How would you allocate these funds?

_____

_____

_____

_____

_____

_____

_____

_____

_____

EXERCISE #17 – UPGRADE YOUR PEER GROUP

If you are really committed to your goal of unleashing the millionaire within you, make sure that you surround yourself with people that you look up to, and that you want to *be* like. Spend your time around positive, confident, successful people, and avoid like the plague negative people.

Whenever I spend time with 8-figure or 9-figure-a-year business owners I feel energized and inspired. It reinforces my belief that "YES, IT **IS** POSSIBLE!" I *can* grow my business to a $10m-a-year venture, sell it on, or even float it on the stock market. After all, *they* did it!

The people you spend time with you become.

The people you surround yourself are either raising your standards or lowering your standards. They are either inspiring you to become the best version of yourself or they encourage you to become a lesser version of yourself.

If you spend time with people that have low self-esteem, no self-confidence, are broke, have low standards for themselves and their lives, and don't focus on creating a magnificent life of abundance and contribution… that is what will happen to *you*. Your own standards will slip, out of a natural desire to be accepted and liked by your peers.

Unfortunately, that's what most people do, because they feel comfortable and unthreatened by people less successful or less confident than *they* are.

Whenever I hang around friends that I grew up with—they are still employees, and their mindset tends to be one of fear, lack, scarcity, 'self-centeredness', and little ambition—I leave feeling drained and disappointed. I love them dearly, and I stay in touch, but they are not people I spend much time with, unless they display a genuine desire to learn and grow. It may sound harsh, or "cold", but you need to weigh this vs how important it is to you to change your life and achieve abundance.

It starts in childhood. Deep down in our subconscious mind we fear that if the people around us don't accept us and love us, we will die.

This is because we relied on the love of our family to survive the first few years of our live. As a result, most people go through life seeking the approval of others, and they don't live their life according to their own, higher values.

Here is how to turn this to your advantage: hang around multi-millionaires and your subconscious mind will *force* you to raise your standards in order to fit in and be accepted by your peers!

I have paid good money for the privilege of seating at the same table as the most successful people in my field. I have paid for mentoring. Without a mentor your very best thinking has got you exactly where you are today, says author Raymond Aaron. I was about to find out just how true this statement is.

Who are the 5 people you spend most time with?

1. _____

2. _____

3. _____

4. _____

5. _____

Are they happy, healthy, and successful? What are their values?

_____

_____

_____

_____

_____

Are the people you currently spend time with *lifting you up* or tearing you down?

_____

_____

_____

Who are the 5 people you know that you want to spend MORE time with?

1. _____

2. _____

3. _____

4. _____

5. _____

* * * * * * * *

A few years ago I organized a week-long retreat for a handful of my coaching clients at a luxurious chalet in the French resort town of Val d'Isère. This would combine three of my favourite things: teaching, skiing, and French food (yes, escargots as well)!

The attendees included three clients who were earning $5,000, $10,000, and $20,000 a month from their business, respectively—having started an online business after attending my seminar—and three clients who had been at the same seminar but who had not made a dime yet.

During breakfast one morning, one of my clients asked me what had been a major turning point in my life. I replied: "Well, completing the '200 reasons why' and '100 ways how' exercises really transformed my mindset very fast."

The client who was earning $20,000 a month from his online 'guitar lessons' business chimed in: "That's true. I started completing those exercises on the same day I got home from your seminar!"

"Me too," said the client earning $5,000 a month. "I started doing them while you were still talking!" added the third successful client.

All three of them who hadn't earned any money yet came clean: they hadn't even **started** working on those exercises...

* * * * * * * *

I hadn't seen or spoken to my father in five years, since I'd left Greece. In truth, I wasn't really on speaking terms with him during my teenage years either, while we all still lived in the same house. His self-esteem issues and decades-long depression and anti-depressant drug abuse made for a toxic living environment.

One of my sisters told me this story:

> "One day I was dancing in the living room with my younger sister, and he walked downstairs, really tired—we'd probably woken him up—and said in a slow, icy tone: 'So... you girls are

happy, eh? You like having fun, eh? Great…. Keep. Doing. That.' And he went to his office to work. We stopped playing immediately and felt really sad and guilty. The belief I've carried with me since that day has been that it's not fair to be happy and to enjoy myself because someone else has to work to pay for this… I feel like a burden… I feel like I'M the burden…

I remember how much I enjoyed going to ballet lessons. It was something that gave me pleasure, as a little girl. But I was always the last kid to pay the fees… It was a burden on dad… because he had to work to pay for it. I was having fun, but it was costing dad. To this day, I can never feel happy, without instantly feeling guilty and bad about it. I even make my husband feel guilty when he enjoys himself, with cutting comments, such as: 'So, you're having fun playing handball with your friends, while I'm taking care of our girls, alone, at home, huh? I could have done with your help here this evening!'"

For many years my sisters and I were workaholics that rarely allowed ourselves to enjoy life. We felt guilty if we were not working *all the time*. My father was extremely proficient at this sort of psychological manipulation. Often, when he felt really depressed, he would come to us or to my mother and utter some cutting remark to put us down. He would *instantly* feel better, relieved to have dragged us down. It was like he needed to feed on our energy like some sort of emotional vampire. This psychological manipulation and emotional abuse went on for years.

While working on Balthazar's exercises I realized it was important to let go of the negativity from the past, forgive, and move on. In that spirit, I called him up, and we agreed to meet up in London. He had been a journalist for 30 years, and was flying over to attend a conference.

Our meeting did not unfold as I expected. When I told him that I had written a 70-page ebook, uploaded it online, and was earning more than $300 a day from its sales thanks to affiliates promoting it, instead of congratulating me and being happy for me, he got angry and dismissive.

"That's not true! It's impossible! Somebody is having you on! It's a scam!", he bellowed. My chest tightened, as I felt hurt and disappointed.

That ebook and the 30 or so variations I'd created would go on to gross more than $2,000,000 in sales. But he could not accept that making money could be so simple. He had worked 16-hour days for thirty years, producing articles that—if bought by newspapers—would earn him $75 to $150 each. The problem was that he had to keep producing new articles all the time. Every day. For thirty years.

The idea of writing something *once* and earning money from it over and over again was alien to him—or at the very least it grated him the wrong way. It would be years before I realized that the more successful I became, the more it reflected back to him his own failures, mistakes, and missed opportunities to fulfil on his potential.

I decided to skip the subject of my newfound success, since it obviously caused him upset, and started talking instead about the personal development seminars I'd been attending. I had managed to lift myself out of my own 8-year bout with depression thanks to the philosophy positive thinking, self-analysis, and self-improvement—the ancient Greeks had talked of 'a healthy mind in a healthy body', after all—and I had hoped to help my father overcome his 30-year addiction to pills and finally find lasting happiness. His reaction was anything but positive.

"This is a CULT! How can you believe such nonsense?! You need to stop all this and get a job! You can write! Why not become a journalist?"

When I tried to make a different point about how we create our reality with our thoughts, our beliefs, and our choices—that we are not 'victims' but rather we are responsible for our life—that is when he really got angry. "OF COURSE I'M A VICTIM! OF COURSE I'M A VICTIM!" he shouted, as he banged his fist on the table. He was too invested in that belief—it was the reality he had built up around him to justify away his failures.

For a few weeks after that meeting with my father I felt very sad, and I sabotaged myself so as to not be more successful than him. It is interesting to note that a lot of men report having their careers and incomes shoot upwards after their fathers pass away—or, alternatively, you can work on such "guilt" issues proactively so as to not let them affect you.

* * * * * * * *

101

Summary – Chapter 2

- ❑ Your invisible world creates your visible world.

- ❑ Your outer world is a reflection of your inner world, and it corresponds to your dominant patterns of thinking. Change your thinking, and you change your life.

- ❑ What really transforms your financial circumstances is adopting a different mindset—the millionaire mindset.

- ❑ Physical reality is the screen that allows us to see our own thinking. If you don't like the movie that is playing… change the *film* (your beliefs).

- ❑ Millionaires know exactly what they want. They have written goals.

- ❑ Money flows from lower value to higher value.

- ❑ If you can just "show up" and produce something you are generally way ahead of 99% of the population.

- ❑ It's never a question of can you do it but rather *will* you do it. It comes down to your degree of motivation and desire.

- ❑ Be determined and committed. Wealth flows to the person who has a high tolerance for uncertainty or disappointment. Handle disappointment well, and you will make more attempts to achieve your goals.

- ❑ THINK BIG and raise your standards. It takes the same amount of energy to think big than to think small.

- ❑ It's a resonation game. You become who you spend time with. Hang out with successful, positive people. Hang out with millionaires.

- ❑ To develop your millionaire mind you must appreciate money. Appreciating money means putting it higher on your value list.

- ❑ Unless you experience a transformation of your values, you won't experience a transformation of your life. With a shift in values comes a shift in destiny.

❑ Unless you have 200 reasons why… you're probably not going to get it.

❑ The Law of Attraction states that what you focus on expands. Focus on the *abundance* all around you, everything you have, and what you are grateful for.

❑ Be grateful for what you *do* have. Remind yourself regularly of all you have to be grateful for and all the abundance in your life.

❑ To those who are GRATEFUL, the Universe will give *more*.

❑ The Universe gives you what you already know you have.

❑ Money is nothing but the measure of the VALUE you create for other people. The more VALUE you create and deliver the more money flows to you.

❑ You can get everything in life you want if you just help enough other people get what they want. Don't chase after the money. Instead, focus on customer acquisition and customer nurturing.

❑ A mission is the best way to meet the most amount of your values, while adding the most amount of value to others.

❑ Money is the manifestation of your resourcefulness.

❑ It is never about resources, it's about resourcefulness.

❑ Be creative and resourceful. Create win-win situations.

❑ Instead of asking yourself "How can I make money…" ask yourself "How can I add 100 Times More Value?"

❑ Writing down 200 reasons why you must earn more money eliminates dozens of limiting beliefs about money, resolves inner conflicts (between your conscious and unconscious), and makes money shoot up in your Hierarchy of Values.

❑ Low self-worth issues, often stemming from childhood, can lead to self-sabotage, self-sacrifice, and subconscious feelings of "Not being good enough" and "Not Deserving". Financial lack can stem from a mind-pattern of low self-worth and self-inflicted punishment (because of feelings of guilt).

❑ Your SELF-WORTH = Your NET WORTH.

103

❑ The secret is… money is not where you think it is. If it was… you'd be rich already. What you have always wanted is inside of you. Wealth, abundance, being rich… is a state of being.

❑ The more you want it the less you have it. Wanting something pushes it away. If you make it about the money, you will fail. It's not about the money.

❑ You become who you spend time with. Surround yourself with positive people that raise your standards.

❑ A lot of successful people plateau and stagnate the second they have accumulated a certain amount of money. They stop working as hard, or saving money as much, because it's not valuable to them... That's why you have to find and devote yourself to a cause that is bigger than you.

CHAPTER 3

Identify & Eliminate Roadblocks

Until you change your thinking, you will keep manifesting the same thing over and over again. You need to go 'upstream' and discover the subconscious beliefs that are creating your current life circumstances. Once you've identified these, you now have a chance at eliminating the limiting beliefs that have been preventing you from achieving true, lasting success.

Thanks to the exercises passed on to me by Balthazar, I was able to identify 44 limiting beliefs that I held about *money* and *wealth*.

For example, I wrote down that "The only way to get rich is to bribe the Greek government!". And: "Rich people are evil, greedy, exploitative. We are good people. that is why we have no money!" (a belief that implies that if you are poor, the people around you will love you and accept you, and if you become rich, you will become the target of people's ire, envy, and resentment).

It became instantly and painfully obvious that these beliefs weren't my own. They had been programmed into my subconscious by my father, a man who had been bouncing from one financial disaster to the next. No wonder I was broke and homeless!

I used these mental exercises to eliminate each of the 44 limiting beliefs, and then programmed my subconscious mind with positive beliefs about myself and money, thanks to a series of 'neuro-linguistic programming' techniques. This radically transformed my mindset and feelings towards wealth, abundance, and success.

28 days later I was earning more than $300 a day in passive income thanks to my website. This would grow within two years to over one million dollars a year in sales.

Your invisible world *truly* creates your visible world.

Identifying Your Limiting Beliefs About Money

The vast majority of people are literally stumbling along blindly, their entire lives, wondering why their lives simply don't work. Health problems... money problems... relationship problems... weight problems... These are just *some* of the symptoms the average person experiences throughout his or her lifetime, because of **conflicting inner programs**.

The things you think you want (consciously) may not be *at all* what you really want (subconsciously). Our subconscious beliefs and fears **drive us significantly more** than our conscious mind does... You see, we create our reality on three levels... Our Thoughts... Our Words... Our Actions. And when our thoughts, words, and actions are aligned, *that* is when things shift powerfully in our physical reality.

Most people go through life sabotaging themselves, with conflicting inner desires. For example, they might think: "I am ready for a beautiful relationship... I want that beautiful Goddess in my life... I can't wait for the connection and the intimacy and sharing and joy together...".

... but in the next moment they think: "*But what if she breaks my heart?!*"

Or, they might consciously believe they "want more money"...

...but actually believe deep down "*my friends won't like me anymore when I make more money than them!*"

106

This sort of 'approach-avoidance' issue is very common. It is a psychological conflict that results from a goal being both desirable and undesirable.

With that in mind, I sat down on that cold, dirty floor with nothing but my journal and a pen, and I started running through an exercise that would identify my 'limiting beliefs about money'. This exercise revealed that I had no less than *44* limiting beliefs about money. These were sabotaging my attempts at every turn. Some of my limiting beliefs included:

❑ "Making money is hard"

❑ "I don't know how to make a lot of money"

❑ "Rich people are evil, greedy, exploitative…"

❑ "If I Make More Money Than People Around Me, They Won't Like Me Anymore."

❑ "What if I fail? Then I'm REALLY a loser…"

❑ "There Isn't Enough Money to Go Around"

❑ "When you have money, spend it quickly, or someone might take it from you!"

❑ "The only way to get rich, is to bribe the Greek government…"

❑ "Money is the root of all evil…"

❑ "Save your money for a rainy day…"

❑ "Money doesn't grow on trees…"

❑ "You can't be rich and spiritual…"

❑ "Money doesn't buy happiness…"

❑ "Money can't buy you love…"

❑ "That's not for people like us…"

❑ "We can't afford it…"

As a result, every time I tried to make money my subconscious mind found subtle ways to have me stop myself, not go all the way, sabotage my success, and ultimately fail. In my subconscious, I feared that *becoming*

107

rich would mean terrible, horrible things for me! It would mean that everyone around me would *hate* me, resent me, despise me, want things from me… I wouldn't be safe!

I remember vividly how my mother would drive us to school in an old, beat-up 20-year-old Communist-era Dacia car manufactured in Romania. There was a hole in the bottom of the chassis, so if you sat at the back you could see the road fly by beneath your feet. I would rage, quietly, at anybody driving along in a nice, fancy, new Mercedes, BMW, or 'Renault Espace'! I literally would wish for *'those mean rich people'* to have their cars topple over on the road. This meant that subconsciously, I was afraid that *other people would wish ill of me*, if I got rich, or if I did better than them. And this is just *one* example of a negative subconscious belief, out of 44.

When I grew up and I worked as a security guard, and then as a telesales agent, I didn't think of these early life experiences *consciously*. But they were still there, *subconsciously*, driving my behaviours, my choices, my decisions.

In my mind **I was linking *pain* to having money and being rich**… ('people will hate me if I'm rich') and **I was linking *pleasure, acceptance, and safety* to *not* having money** ('my friends will like me more if I am broke, like <u>they</u> are!').

I have coached hundreds of people all over the world on this topic and helped them dramatically increase their income. Some of their limiting beliefs about money included:

- ❑ "You have to be born wealthy, to be a millionaire…"
- ❑ "I'm not educated enough…"
- ❑ "It takes luck to be a millionaire" [actually, it takes focus, work, and the right mindset]
- ❑ "You have to be a crook to get rich…"
- ❑ "I'm too old to start…"
- ❑ "It's hard to make money… money doesn't grow on trees…"
- ❑ "To make money you have to take advantage of other people…"

- ❑ "To get rich you have to take it from someone else, and they'll have less. It's not fair."

- ❑ "I can't afford to start my own business…"

- ❑ "What if I fail? What will people think of me? I'll be ridiculed!"

- ❑ "What if I make a lot of money and lose it all? Then I'm really a failure!"

- ❑ "I'm afraid…what if I fail?!!" ("…then I'm really not good enough!")

- ❑ "I am afraid of rejection. What if people say no? What if people don't like my product?"

- ❑ "If I make more money than my friends they won't like me anymore."

- ❑ "It's not fair that some people have more than others… so I'll remain poor…"

- ❑ "I'm not good enough. I don't deserve more money and happiness."

- ❑ "All the good ideas are taken…"

- ❑ "People fight over money, so it is better to not have any."

- ❑ "Money Is The Root Of All Evil… so it's better if I don't have any…"

- ❑ "In order to make more money I'll have to work harder and I won't have time to enjoy it, so why even try?"

- ❑ "To make money you need to be really smart, and I'm not smart enough…"

- ❑ "Money doesn't buy you happiness… money can't buy you love."

- ❑ "If I make a lot of money I'll get sucked in. what about my spiritual side?"

- ❑ "If I get rich, everyone's going to want a handout…"

- ❑ "Others need it more than me. I don't deserve it…"

- ❑ "I'm afraid about money because… I've had it in the past and lost it. I don't want to experience that again."

109

❏ "I feel GUILTY about having a better life than my mother."

❏ "Having too much is a bad thing… you'll be 'spoilt rotten'…"

❏ "Look at those uneducated people who made a lot of money suddenly in Poland… they still have hay sticking out their shoes… They're probably drug dealers…"

❏ "I am comfortable and satisfied with having just enough to get by… like my mom…"

❏ "Money goes to people who are materialistic and lack human qualities, screwing people along the way!"

❏ "Making $1,000,000 a year is IMPOSSIBLE! … It scares me!"

❏ "I am afraid about money because it goes as quick as it comes…"

Brian Tracy says: "Your outer world is a reflection of your inner world, and it corresponds to your dominant patterns of thinking. **Change your thinking, and you will change your life**." Author T. Harv Eker adds: "Lack of money is never a problem. It is a result. If a problem exists, it's in your thinking and how that thinking manifests through feelings and actions to produce your results. It is the result of conditioned and largely automatic thinking."

If you have a relationship filled with anger, resentment, guilt, fear, etc. would it grow and blossom? Negative statements about money, overheard while still a child, might still be determining your financial life and destiny. These are the main reason why people are not doing well financially, or why they sabotage themselves when they finally achieve success.

With that said, let's begin exploring your subconscious…

EXERCISE #18 – IDENTIFY YOUR LIMITING BELIEFS

What did your father, mother, family member, or teacher say to you that negatively impacted your self-esteem?

_____

_____

_____

_____

_____

_____

Do you remember a specific emotionally significant incident that affected your view of yourself?

_____

_____

_____

_____

_____

_____

Complete this sentence: The worst thing about me is…

_____

_____

_____

_____

_____

_____

I don't like myself because…

_____

_____

_____

_____

I don't like myself when I…

_____

_____

_____

_____

I sometimes feel I am not good enough because…

_____

_____

_____

_____

Other people don't like me because…

_____

_____

_____

_____

_____

I can't succeed in life because…

_____

_____

_____

_____

_____

I feel unhappy about myself because…

_____

_____

_____

_____

_____

113

I feel guilty because…

_____

_____

_____

_____

_____

I feel sad because…

_____

_____

_____

_____

_____

I feel ashamed because…

_____

_____

_____

_____

I feel afraid because...

_____

_____

_____

_____

_____

I feel angry because...

_____

_____

_____

_____

Where in your life are you limiting yourself?

_____

_____

_____

_____

_____

115

Where in your life do you feel you have little to no self worth?

_____

_____

_____

_____

Where do you feel overwhelmed? Where are you doing too much?

_____

_____

_____

_____

Why are you doing so much in that area? What are you trying to compensate or hide?

_____

_____

_____

_____

"Your money is simply an outgrowth or representation symbolically of your mind pattern. Financial lack is a way of affirming these negative mind-patterns. Determine where this all began. Do your Release Work. Let go of the negative space-holders so the positive ones have room to manifest."

Stewart Swerdlow, *Stewart Says*

Where in life are you stagnating?

_____

_____

_____

_____

_____

_____

Who do you feel abandoned by?

_____

_____

_____

_____

_____

What conflicts come up in your relationships with other people—spouse, partner, business partner, men, women, colleagues, employees, neighbours—over and over again, in the course of your life?

_____

_____

_____

_____

_____

117

EXERCISE #19 – IDENTIFY YOUR LIMITING BELIEFS ABOUT MONEY

Complete these sentences and/or answer the following questions. Write down three or four answers for each. Do not edit or censor your subconscious mind; write down whatever comes to you as an answer, even if it doesn't make sense to you in the moment:

The worst thing about money is…

_____

_____

_____

_____

_____

I can't make a lot of money because…

_____

_____

_____

_____

_____

I can't earn $30,000 a month because…

_____

_____

_____

_____

_____

_____

I can't earn $1,000,000 a year because...

_____

_____

_____

_____

_____

How were your parents in the area of money? Were they entrepreneurs or employees? Were they investors? Were they good with money?

_____

_____

_____

_____

_____

_____

What did you hear about money, growing up? What sentences do you remember?

_____

_____

_____

_____

_____

_____

Do you remember a specific emotionally significant incident regarding money?

_____

_____

_____

_____

_____

_____

In the area of 'money' I feel **afraid** because...

_____

_____

_____

_____

_____

_____

_____

_____

_____

_____

_____

In the area of 'money' I feel **angry** because…

_____

_____

_____

_____

_____

_____

_____

_____

_____

_____

In the area of 'money' I feel **ashamed** because…

_____

_____

_____

_____

_____

_____

In the area of 'money' I feel **guilty** because…

_____

_____

_____

_____

_____

Having completed the questions above, what would you say are your 3 main limiting beliefs or fears about money?

1) _____

2) _____

3) _____

How To Eliminate Your Limiting Beliefs

Already, the act of having identified a limiting belief (and writing it down on paper) begins the process of removing it from your subconscious mind. Why? Firstly, because when you write down that limiting belief, you often realize where it originates from—and quickly understand that it doesn't originate from you; it wasn't your choice.

One of my limiting beliefs about money used to be:

"You only get rich by bribing the Greek government!"

I had never thought that consciously, personally! My father had! And yet, it was there, lodged in my subconscious.

Secondly, the act of writing down your limiting belief on paper EXTERIORIZES that sentiment or belief. It is now literally 'outside of you'. You can look at that sentence on that piece of paper and decide whether you want it to remain a part of you or not.

There are a number of ways to eliminate a limiting belief. Once you have elicited a limiting belief, write down the exact opposite belief. Then, write down five to ten reasons why this <u>new</u> belief is TRUE.

You see, our BELIEFS are like a table-top. They are supported by 'legs' that consist of our past experiences that act as reference points. To collapse a limiting belief, you need to "sweep away" the legs that support it.

Making a lot of money is HARD…

Making a lot of money is FUN and EASY!

There are five ways to do so.

The first way involves asking yourself why you believe this. Reflect upon your life and write down every experience you had that reinforced this belief. Try to trace this back to the earliest experience from where this belief emerged. Gather any evidence that suggests this belief is false. Can you think of any real life examples when a statement like this was not true? Can you think of any examples in your life where this statement about yourself was false?

Then, write down *the opposite* belief, and write down the reasons why each new, *opposite* belief is true. Your mind cannot hold on to two conflicting or contradictory beliefs.

EXERCISE #20 – EXERCISE OF OPPOSITES

Remember the limiting beliefs that you uncovered? Now write down your new, positive and empowering *opposite* beliefs, and five reasons why each of these new beliefs is TRUE:

NEW BELIEF #1)

_____

Why is this new belief true?

_____

_____

_____

_____

_____

NEW BELIEF #2)

_____

Why is this new belief true?

_____

_____

_____

_____

_____

NEW BELIEF #3)

_____

Why is this new belief true?

_____

_____

_____

_____

_____

NEW BELIEF #4)

_____

Why is this new belief true?

_____

125

_____

_____

_____

_____

NEW BELIEF #5)

_____

Why is this new belief true?

_____

_____

_____

_____

_____

NEW BELIEF #6)

_____

Why is this new belief true?

_____

_____

_____

_____

_____

NEW BELIEF #7)

_____

Why is this new belief true?

_____

_____

_____

_____

_____

NEW BELIEF #8)

_____

Why is this new belief true?

_____

_____

_____

_____

_____

EXERCISE #21 – REWRITE THE PAST

In this exercise you will rewrite negative experiences from your past, relating to your financial goal, into a new story with a wonderful, positive outcome, as if everything turned out great. This teaches your unconscious what you *really* want. It also helps reframe your negative experiences, in your subconscious mind. And thirdly, it will help you refine your goal-setting work by clarifying exactly *how* you want the money to show up in your life.

Let me give you a couple examples from my own life.

In 2006 my business soared from a turnover of £120,000 the previous year to £1,160,000—almost a ten-fold increase in sales. But we were owed over £100,000 in installments, clients weren't paying up, my team was wasting their time chasing them up, business partners were upset because they weren't getting paid their commissions on time, I felt hurt by their comments, and on top of everything I was working 16 hours a day and my relationship and health were suffering.

So I rewrote this story. Here is an extract of what I wrote:

> "£1,160,000 flooded into my life and into my bank accounts, and all my attendees, clients, speakers, and joint venture partners were thrilled and delighted with the value they received. Everyone was paid on time and equitably, according to the value they contributed. My staff and my systems were outstanding, allowing me to only work three days a week."

Doing this 'rewrite' helped clarify for me *how* I want to receive large amounts of money: with good feelings all around, and with excellent support around me.

In 2013 my seminars generated $1.7m in sales in twelve weeks. But I felt stressed and unhappy from having to coach 110 clients for over a year (60 of them had paid $25,000 each) and I felt I didn't have the time to do the things I really wanted to do with my time.

So I rewrote the story:

"I loved travelling around the world, sharing my message, connecting with people, and inspiring people. All my clients, attendees, and business partners were thrilled and delighted with the value they received. I shared what makes my heart sing. The programs sold delivered massive value while requiring little to none of my time."

Doing this rewrite again helped me clarify *how* I want to receive large amounts of money: selling programs and products that deliver massive value while requiring little to none of my time to deliver them (thanks to systems, courses, and coaches that I have trained to work in my stead).

Doing this exercise helps to dissipate the emotional charge of those negative experiences relating to receiving large amounts of money, and it helped me clarify exactly *how* I wanted the money to show up in my life.

Your turn now…

Write down the following.

What was a negative experience you had, relating to money?

_____

_____

_____

How would you rewrite this story with an ideal, wonderful outcome?

_____

_____

_____

_____

_____

_____

What was another negative experience you had, relating to money?

_____

_____

_____

How would you rewrite this story with an ideal, wonderful outcome?

_____

_____

_____

_____

_____

What was a third negative experience relating to money or business in general?

_____

_____

_____

How would you rewrite this story with an ideal, wonderful outcome?

_____

_____

_____

_____

_____

_____

What was a negative experience relating to making or receiving a lot of money?

_____

_____

_____

How would you rewrite this story with an ideal, wonderful outcome?

_____

_____

_____

_____

_____

_____

What was a fourth negative experience relating to money?

_____

_____

_____

_____

How would you rewrite this story with an ideal, wonderful outcome?

_____

_____

_____

_____

_____

_____

EXERCISE #22 – WHY YOU <u>CAN</u> SUCCEED

Write down 20 reasons why you CAN succeed!

1) _____

2) _____

3) _____

4) _____

5) _____

6) _____

7) _____

8) _____

9) _____

10) _____

11) _____

12) _____

13) _____

14) _____

15) _____

16) _____

17) _____

18) _____

19) _____

20) _____

EXERCISE #23 – NO MORE APPROVAL-SEEKING

Write down 20 reasons why it doesn't matter what anyone else thinks or says about you pursuing your dreams, least of all your parents:

1) _____

2) _____

3) _____

4) _____

5) _____

6) _____

7) _____

8) _____

9) _____

10) _____

11) _____

12) _____

13) _____

14) _____

15) _____

16) _____

17) _____

18) _____

19) _____

20) _____

Examples include:

- ❏ "I follow my dreams no matter what, because no one else will do it for me!"

- ❏ "I follow my dreams no matter what, because I don't want the regret of not having gone for it, when I'm in my 90s!"

- ❏ "I don't let other people's fears, prejudices, manipulation, or agendas determine what I do with my life! Only I know what I am truly capable of, and what I am truly meant to do with my life!"

- ❏ "I don't need to do things to gain approval from other, because I approve of myself!"

- ❏ "If I don't follow my passion, follow my dreams, and live out my TRUE LIFE MISSION then thousands of people around the world will suffer, because I haven't helped them!"

- ❏ "I MUST follow my dreams and my mission, because it is truly a sin to waste so much potential for doing good!"

EXERCISE #24 – WHY YOU DESERVE WEALTH

Write down 20 reasons why you DESERVE great wealth, happiness, success, and the finer things in life:

1) _____
2) _____
3) _____
4) _____
5) _____
6) _____
7) _____
8) _____
9) _____
10) _____
11) _____
12) _____
13) _____
14) _____
15) _____
16) _____
17) _____
18) _____
19) _____
20) _____

EXERCISE #25 – THE 'NO NEED TO STRUGGLE' EXERCISE

Write down 20 reasons why money will flow to you easily, gracefully, in oceans of abundance, without the need for struggle:

1) _____

2) _____

3) _____

4) _____

5) _____

6) _____

7) _____

8) _____

9) _____

10) _____

11) _____

12) _____

13) _____

14) _____

15) _____

16) _____

17) _____

18) _____

19) _____

20) _____

EXERCISE #26 – MAKING MONEY IS FUN & EASY

Write down 20 reasons why making money is FUN and EASY!

1) _____

2) _____

3) _____

4) _____

5) _____

6) _____

7) _____

8) _____

9) _____

10) _____

11) _____

12) _____

13) _____

14) _____

15) _____

16) _____

17) _____

18) _____

19) _____

20) _____

EXERCISE #27 – YOU <u>ARE</u> GOOD ENOUGH

Write down 20 reasons why OF COURSE people will want to hear what you have to say, read your book, attend your seminar, or buy from your company:

1) _____

2) _____

3) _____

4) _____

5) _____

6) _____

7) _____

8) _____

9) _____

10) _____

11) _____

12) _____

13) _____

14) _____

15) _____

16) _____

17) _____

18) _____

19) _____

20) _____

EXERCISE #28 – THERE IS **NO** COMPE-TITION

Optional exercise for authors, experts, coaches, consultants, therapists: Write down 20 reasons why it doesn't matter how much competition there is or how many other people are already talking about your topic.

1) _____

2) _____

3) _____

4) _____

5) _____

6) _____

7) _____

8) _____

9) _____

10) _____

11) _____

12) _____

13) _____

14) _____

15) _____

16) _____

17) _____

18) _____

19) _____

20) _____

Other Techniques For Eliminating Limiting Beliefs

Other techniques for eliminating negative or limiting beliefs include the "scrambler" technique (a Neuro-Linguistic Programming tool that involves repeating the fear or limiting belief in a funny mickey-mouse-like high-pitched voice, for example), or Emotional Freedom Technique (EFT, also known as 'Tapping'). The concept here is that a belief in one's mind is like a groove in a vinyl record. If you 'scratch' that groove in the 'record' over and over again, it will no longer be able to 'play' that pattern. The message becomes 'scrambled'.

Other techniques I have used—and continue to use to this day—for eliminating limiting beliefs and reprogramming the mind include:

- Affirmations
- Visualization
- Hypnosis
- Subliminal software
- Emotional Freedom Technique (EFT)

I also find that immersion in wealth building education (reading books and listening to audio programs about successful wealth creators, attending seminars and retreats, etc.) "flood" my subconscious mind with positive beliefs about money and success. This helps eliminate those limiting beliefs even more.

Modelling the beliefs of rich and successful people is a great way to get started with reprogramming your mind for achieving success (see list of empowering beliefs in Chapter 2).

* * * * * * * * *

It took me three whole days to complete the mindset exercises that Balthazar had assigned. By brainstorming '100 ways how' I had come up with an idea that I got very excited and enthusiastic about. By writing down '200 reasons why' I had all the motivation in the world. By identifying and eliminating my limiting beliefs about money, I no longer had conflicting 'inner desires' and no longer sabotaged myself. I took action immediately, without procrastinating or being overcome by fear.

Less than a month later I launched my first business, on the Internet, which started bringing in $300 a day. Everything I touched turned to gold—all of a sudden I had the Midas touch. By my second year in business, I was generating $400,000 a year in passive income and earning twice as much from running seminars.

* * * * * * * *

I launched my first book in 2012, highlighting some of my marketing strategies, and it became a New York Times Bestseller and a Wall Street Journal bestseller. I started receiving hundreds of emails a day, from people desperate to change their financial situation… Emails like these:

> "Hi Mark. I'm facing eviction. If you had to pick just 1 idea from the book to make fast cash in the next 3 weeks what would it be?" — Darren T.

> "Hi Mark, I am out of work, with 2 small kids. My husband is unable to work due to a medical condition. I need to act fast…What is the quickest way to get started and make some income?" — Veronica

> "Hello Mark, we have accumulated $80,000 in debt. We are fighting to keep our home. My wife works 2 jobs and I work a second job part time. I am 60 years old and I cannot see any way to ever retiring. Can someone guide us through the steps?" — Frank T.

> "Hi Mark, I'm a 52-year-old dad with 4 kids, two of which still live at home. A few months ago my wife decided she didn't want to be a wife or mother any longer, so after cleaning out the bank accounts and not paying bills for a few months and putting our home in foreclosure she went back to Indiana

where she is from. I own a small cleaning company, but the economy and the fact I've lost the use of my right arm has made that kind of work difficult. Do you know of a good program for a "newbie" to use to make some quick cash?" — Mike A.

Everyone was asking me the same question: how to make money fast and easy. I tried replying that they had to work on their mindset, first, before exploring the opportunities available to them, but this advice was met with a stony silence.

Very few people, it seemed, were ready to hear that they had to take responsibility for their thinking. They were looking for a solution or opportunity that was "outside" of them... It was far too appealing to go along with the idea that they were victims of circumstance.

And then one day I received the following email by a man who would later become a close friend—Bishop Stewart:

"Hi Mark, I have always been a very passionate entrepreneur and had built up a few successful companies. I could immediately relate to your story of being homeless. When I was young, at one point I ran away from home and slept on the roofs of people's houses to avoid getting mugged at night.

Then I did what nobody believed I could... I built a multi-million-dollar company from scratch, rapidly growing it to 24 employees and millions of dollars in sales within a year. Everyone said I couldn't start a company since I didn't go to college, but I built it anyway. I have always believed in being an entrepreneur and owning your own life.

And then suddenly things changed. I lost it all, in so many ways. At first I wasn't worried about it, because I usually bounce right back. But not this time.

I knew it wasn't the economy because I've never believed in that kind of thinking. I've always been a very positive person. I believe 100% in taking FULL responsibility in life. We are the architects of our own destiny. That was the frustrating part. I

143

couldn't figure it out to save my life. It was like every penny was running from me.

I was really down because while I am the youngest in the family, I had employed my older brothers when they lost their jobs, and so many people depended on me. I was frustrated and depressed. I would see other people doing well and I couldn't figure out what was causing this slump, and why I couldn't break through it. My marriage ended, I lost my business, and there was a rift with family members. My whole life had turned upside down. Before, everything I touched turned to gold, and suddenly everything was failing and my life was going downhill… I had days I would just yell out loud "What am I missing?! GOD, HELP ME!"

That is when I came across your "21 Millionaire Mindset Secrets" book. I read your book, took out a journal, and did all the exercises in it. I realized quickly, that I was manifesting all of this. It hit me like a ton of bricks. I knew this was the answer. It was my inner world that was creating my outer world. I read that in your course and wrote it down and hung it up. I looked at it everyday, **to remind me that I have control over what is happening in my life** and I am the cause of it. I made so many huge discoveries about myself while doing your exercises!

It made me shed many tears to bring up things from the past, and past hurts… It was so powerful to realize the reason I lost everything and WHY it wasn't coming back so easily. I had all of this 'bad programming' and limiting beliefs that were making me self-sabotage myself every time I reached a certain point.

One of the most powerful things I realized was that **I had started to hate money, subconsciously**. I had stopped caring about my business. Deep down, I resented it. Why? Because I had started to feel like everyone just wanted to get money out of me. I would go to church every Sunday and people would come up to me and ask me for money. My brother and I had a huge falling out due to money (this really made me feel "used"). Similar situations with so many other important people in my life made me start hating money… My mindset had changed… I had begun to resent and hate money without even realizing it.

Immediately after completing your exercises everyone began to notice a difference in me. I had so many people say "wow, Bishop is back". I would ask them what do they mean and they would say things like "We can just see a change in your eyes and spirit… there's been a shift in you… your energy within is back!"

Ideas were pouring out of me and new business opportunities presented themselves to me again. Your book changed my life for the better and exposed me to myself in a powerful way. . I can't thank you enough. I am looking forward to great things and I appreciate all the great material you provide. I understand the power of wise counsel and great mentors... so thank you for being mine."

This email showed me I was on the right track. I decided it was time to share these insights with more people…

* * * * * * * * *

Summary – Chapter 3

- ❏ The real reason why most people fail is their fears and their limiting beliefs.

- ❏ Your money is simply an outgrowth or representation symbolically of your mind pattern.

- ❏ Financial lack is a way of affirming negative mind-patterns.

- ❏ Many people are broke because deep down they "hate" or are afraid of money.

- ❏ Many people who come into a lot of money are uncomfortable with it at a subconscious level and therefore sabotage themselves.

- ❏ Do not think like a 'business opportunity seeker'. Instead, think like a self-made entrepreneur.

- ❏ Most people won't do it... because it takes personal responsibility.

- ❏ The exercises in this section will help you align your subconscious with your conscious desires.

CHAPTER 4

Reprogram Your Mind

Now that you have worked diligently at eliminating limiting beliefs from your mind, it is time to program your mind with new, *positive* images and beliefs. I will be teaching you in this chapter how to use:

- ❏ Affirmations
- ❏ Visualization
- ❏ Hypnosis
- ❏ Subliminal Technology
- ❏ The Power of Feelings
- ❏ The Power of Intention
- ❏ Your Daily Power Regimen

These are the techniques I continue to use to this day—to design and create my life as I want it.

Mind Programming Technique #1: Affirmations

Affirmations, spoken with feeling (excitement, gratitude, joy), are incredibly powerful in manifesting a desired reality. FEEL the excitement of being that which you are affirming. When I say "I inspire millions of people around the world", or "I Love My Life!" I imagine myself on stage in front of thousands of people, feeling thrilled, excited, and grateful!

I start my day by saying my affirmations ten to twenty-one times each, out loud, with excitement in my voice, as I visualize the outcome. Some of my favourite affirmations include:

- ❑ I Am Amazing! I Am Inspiration! I Am Power!

- ❑ I Am a Genius and I Apply My Wisdom! I have access to all the wisdom that I need!

- ❑ I Love My Life! I Am Rich, I Am Loved, I Am Grateful!

- ❑ Every Day, In Every Way, I Am Healthier & Stronger!

- ❑ Every Day In Every Way I Am Better & Better!

- ❑ Every Day In Every Way I Am More Efficient & Productive!

- ❑ I Express Myself Freely and Creatively! I Inspire Millions of People Around The World!

- ❑ Money Flows To Me In Avalanches of Abundance, From All Directions, And I Am Grateful Beyond Measure For All The Abundance, Love, and Joy in my Life!

- ❑ I expand in abundance, success & love every day as I inspire those around me to do the same!

"You get your life to "take off" by first becoming very clear in your thinking about it. When your thoughts are clear and steadfast, begin to speak them as truths. Say them out loud. Use the great command that calls forth creative power: I AM. Make I-am statements to others. "I am" is the strongest creative statement in the universe. Whatever you think, whatever you say, after the words "I am" sets into motion those experiences, calls them forth, brings them to you. There is no other way the Universe knows how to work. There is no other route it knows to take. The Universe responds to "I am" as would a genie in a bottle."

Neale Donald Walsch, *Conversations With God*

You see, we create on three levels: Thought. Word. Deed.

❑ Your thoughts are creative... Your thoughts are an energy that goes on forever.

❑ Your words *are even more creative*. You are bringing the world of the invisible (your thoughts) into physical reality, through the physical vibration of *sound*. Writing down your thoughts is also a very powerful process of creation (it makes your thoughts more real, tangible, and concrete; this is another reason why writing down our goals in a journal is so important).

❑ And finally, your ACTIONS (or 'deeds') are the physical embodiment of your thoughts and your words.

When your thoughts, words, and actions are *aligned*, you become a powerful CREATOR. The problem is, most people are completely out of integrity with themselves. What they think, what they say, and what they *do* are very different. For example:

(thought) *"Hmm... I should go on a diet...*
(said aloud) *"I am going on a diet!*
(action taken) *"I'll start my diet after I finish this chocolate cake..."*

Create Your New Life Thanks To Affirmations

A thought that is spoken over and over again, thousands of times, has incredible creative power to it. it gets seared in your brain as a new neuro-association. A new belief is formed. A word expressed over and over again becomes just that – expressed, pushed out. It eventually becomes your physical reality. Remember: You are a very powerful creator!

> "By repeating an affirmation over and over again, it becomes embedded in the subconscious mind, and eventually becomes your reality. That is why you need to be careful what you think and believe, because that is exactly what you will get!"
>
> Anthony Robbins

Some of the positive affirmations contained in my Prosperity Power™ subliminal software (available at www.LifeCanBeAwesome.com) include:

I am successful
I love my life and I am grateful
I know exactly what I want
I achieve all I want
I am a genius and I apply my wisdom
I attract success effortlessly
Every day in every way I am more and more successful
I express myself freely and creatively
I am an amazing success
I am a powerful creator
I always make the right decisions
I am grateful for my wealth and prosperity
I am wealthy, I am loved, I am grateful
I love and accept myself
I am congratulated for my achievements
Money flows to me in oceans of abundance
Making money is fun and easy
I attract money effortlessly
Every day in every way I am richer and richer
Every day in every way I am healthier and stronger
My wealth increases as I create more abundance for all to enjoy
I enjoy my wealth and I have fun
Money comes easily to me
My income is constantly increasing
I am a money magnet
I enjoy making money
Prosperity of all kinds is drawn to me
Money flows to me from unexpected sources
I accept abundance in my life now
My good comes from everywhere and everyone
I am a business genius
My business is thriving
I attract thousands of customers effortlessly
Our customers are raving fans of our business
I am a powerful creator
I am a powerful business leader
The right opportunities to increase my income open up for me now

EXERCISE #29 – YOUR AFFIRMATIONS

Write down your 10 new affirmations:

1) _____

2) _____

3) _____

4) _____

5) _____

6) _____

7) _____

8) _____

9) _____

10) _____

Note: Repeat your affirmations out loud 21 times each, every day, with the feeling and emotion of **unbridled excitement, gratitude, and joy!** Why gratitude, excitement, and joy? Because these are the emotions that ATTRACT abundance *to* you… and you are thanking the "Universe" for what has already been created and manifested in your reality! Thank you!

Mind Programming Technique #2: Visualization

Visualization is a well-known technique for goal-achievement and performance enhancement, supported by substantial scientific evidence. It is used by some of the most successful people in the world, be it world-class athletes or billionaire business owners.

There is tremendous creative power in visualizing clearly and exactly that image of what you want to create in your life. There are many reasons why this technique is so powerful. Firstly, clarity is power. Sending out such a precise, clear thought into the Universe aligns you "vibrationally" with that outcome. In other words, you start resonating at the same frequency as that 'picture' (that precise outcome) in your mind.

Secondly, your brain won't resist you as much. Your brain is not there to 'make you happy'; it's there to protect you, to keep you in the 'comfort zone' that you've gotten used to. If your brain has "seen" that new outcome over and over again, it will interpret it as "real"—an outcome that has already occurred—so it will no longer be outside your comfort zone or scary. Your brain must 'see it before it can believe it'.

Visualizing our perfect outcome creates a new neural pathway that primes our mind and our body to act in a way that is consistent with the achievement of that image, vastly increasing your chances of achieving and experiencing it.

> "See yourself enjoying the achievement of your goal. Feel like it's already done! It's yours! It will then manifest into your life."
>
> Earl Nightingale, *The Strangest Secret*

The Greek shipping magnate Onassis would rehearse in his head over and over again how he wanted his business meetings to turn out. Like a sorcerer, he would have the most hardened businessmen who'd turned down dozens of other similar proposals saying yes to everything he wanted within moments of meeting him. I have done this many, many times. It really works like magic!

One of the reasons why visualization and 'mental rehearsals' work so well is because they help our minds turn the 'unfamiliar' and scary (things that are outside our comfort zone) into the *familiar*.

Every day I visualize thousands of grateful people from around the world handing me envelopes filled with money, and I am gratefully accepting all this abundance, feeling *grateful* for it flowing to me. I visualize my many bank accounts steadily growing in wealth, day after day, as I find new and better ways to reach more people and help them improve their life. I visualize myself living my ideal life, in my dream home, experiencing my "Perfect Day".

I also visualize myself giving a powerful talk to thousands of people at packed seminars around the world; I visualize their positive and grateful reactions and their love flowing towards me! I visualize thousands of people rushing to buy my books and avidly reading them, with glee and delight, and raving about them to their friends! I visualize myself in an endless room filled with every kind of abundance and material thing that I can imagine. I have no doubt. I just KNOW that it is so.

My daily visualization routine also includes visualizing:

- PALE PINK around me and throughout me for unconditional love for myself.
- ICE BLUE in my Thyroid Area (to unblock my communication)
- I breathe in MEDIUM GREEN in my Heart Chakra area, and blow out Red (anger), Grey (emotional confusion), and **Blue (isolation).**
- I do the **"CHILD WITHIN"** and "GOLDEN ALTAR" visualizations/release work, daily.
- The POWER ARCHETYPE in every cell of my body: 𝝠
- The "Chakra Spinning" exercise and the "Ultimate Protection Technique" visualization.

Visualization Activates The Law of Attraction

Jack Canfield, co-author of the Chicken Soup For The Soul series, relates the story of how his mentor W. Clement Stone wanted him to set a goal so big that it would PROVE to Jack that what he was teaching at his seminar really worked. What did Stone teach? The power of visualisation, affirmations, perseverance, and taking inspired action (listening to your inner voice through meditation).

Jack was earning $8,000 a year at the time, as a Chicago public school teacher. He decided to set a huge goal for himself: to earn $100,000 in a year. He had no idea how he could possibly to do that—this represented a 12-fold increase in his annual income!

Undaunted, he proceeded to follow Stone's teachings. He created the image of a $100,000 cheque on a big piece of paper, and stuck it on his ceiling so that he could visualise it every night and every morning.

Canfield goes on to say:

> "Everything can change in your life when you change your thinking of what is possible. Success lies just outside your comfort zone. How do you get comfortable with concepts you are uncomfortable about, such as self-promotion or earning a six-figure income? Through visualization. **Visualisation is the most powerful tool for the transformation of conscious-ness, and the activation of the Law of Attraction,** and for coming up with the creative solutions for your problems. You'll start perceiving things you've never perceived before."

Shortly thereafter an idea came to him: "If I sell 400,000 copies of my book on self-esteem, at 25 cents per copy in royalties, that's $100,000!" By focusing his mind on this outcome he achieved his goal of earning one hundred thousand dollars that very year!

Together with his co-author Mark Victor Hansen, they would later create a "visionboard" of one hundred million copies of their "Chicken Soup" book, next to a bowl of actual chicken soup, Mark, Jack, and the TV show host Oprah Winfrey superimposed on that image. It took an entire wall at their publicist's office and at their own offices, so that they could visualize their goal every day—and it worked! The *Chicken Soup For The Soul* series has sold over 100 million copies worldwide to date!

Visual Reminders

In my house I have silver bowls filled with coins and other symbols of wealth spread around, as a visual reminder of the abundance that flows through my life. I also have the words 'Love & Gratitude' stuck on our glass water bottles as well as on the fridge. In my office I have three visionboards, one 'HeroBoard' of people who inspire me, and two 'gratitude boards' (pictures of happy times with Mira, our children, and our loved ones).

Your Turn

Describe in detail on the following pages how you want your life to turn out. Create a detailed mental image of the desired outcome using all of your senses. What do you see around you? Where are you? What do you look like? Who is around you? What do you hear people say? What are you feeling grateful for? What are you feeling incredibly proud of?

Envision yourself achieving your goal. Imagine the finest details of what you would love to achieve. The greater the detail you can envision, the more power you have to create. Feel the feelings and emotions this achievement would bring you. <u>The four most powerful creative feelings, incidentally, are those of gratitude, love, inspiration, and enthusiasm.</u>

Play a mental movie in your head, then see yourself getting into that movie! Mentally rehearse it again and again and again! Absolutely EXPECT it to happen. Make the picture big and bright! Put yourself in the picture! See your ideal self smiling and being happy! What do you hear? What do you smell? What do you see? Who is around you? Feel what you would feel if these goals were already yours! Get excited!

By concentrating on this visualization for 5 straight minutes every day, you are burning an imprint of it on your subconscious mind, and it will go to work immediately to bring to you anything and everything you desire. This works like *magic*.

"I have established Laws in the universe that make it possible for you to have – to create – exactly what you choose. These Laws cannot be violated, nor can they be ignored. You cannot not follow the Law, for these are the ways things work. You cannot step aside from this; you cannot operate outside of it. [...] The Laws are very simple: Thought is creative. Fear attracts like energy. Love is all there is. [...] The process of creation starts with thought. Nothing exists in your world that did not first exist as pure thought. [...] I gave all My spirit children the same power to create which I have as the whole. Our essence is the same. We are the "same stuff"! With all the same properties and abilities – including the ability to create physical reality out of thin air."

Neale Donald Walsch, Conversations With God

68 Seconds of Pure Thought

"We encourage you to act a little bit less, and envision a little bit more. There is power in lining up energy. When you hold that thought purely (i.e. a non- contradictive thought) for as little 17 seconds, another thought of the same vibrational equivalent—because of the Law of Attraction—joins it. When these two thoughts come together, there is an EXPLOSION of energy. In order to give you an idea of the power of the thought, we would say to you: When that first 17 seconds joins, there is an energy expansion that is equivalent to 2,000 action-hours. That's huge. When you cross the next 17-second mark, the expression of energy is 10 times the first: 20,000 action-hours. When you hold it for the third sequence of 17 seconds... another ten times. Each time there is another 17 seconds of non-contradiction, the thought catapults into a whole new level. So that 68 seconds of pure thought has HUGE action-consequences. That is why we say that one who is connected to Source is many, many times more powerful than one who is not, because there is no self-defeating that is going on."

Abraham-Hicks

156

All Success Begins With Definiteness of Purpose
and a Clear Picture In Your Mind

"Let me call your attention to a great power which is under your control," said Mr. Carnegie, "the power which is greater than poverty, greater than the lack of education, greater than all of your fears and superstitions combined. It is the power to take possession of your own mind and direct it toward whatever end you may desire. This profound power, is the gift of the Creator, and it must have been considered the greatest of all of his gifts to man, because it is the only thing over which man has the complete and unchallengeable right of control and direction."

"When you speak of your poverty and your lack of education," Mr. Carnegie explained, "you are simply directing your mind power to attract these undesirable circumstances. Because it is true that whatever your mind feeds upon, your mind attracts to you. Now you see why it is important that you recognize that all success begins with definiteness of purpose, with a clear picture in your mind of precisely what you want from life."

Napoleon Hill, *Think And Grow Rich*

"Visualize what you would love. The more detail you can envision, the more power you have. You are a co-creator, and the more vision and visualization you have, the greater your power to create. Imagine the finest details of what you would love to see. Can you see that any questions or obstacles that you might have are exactly the details you leave out? In much the same way, your uncertainty in life is directly proportionate to the details that you haven't questioned and answered. If you want to achieve self-mastery, you must ask the questions and get the details to master your life or you won't build it. The question is, are you important enough to yourself to take the time to plan?"

John Demartini, *The Breakthrough Experience*

EXERCISE #30 – YOUR DAILY VISUALIZATION ROUTINE

Write down your daily visualization routine:

_____

_____

_____

_____

_____

_____

_____

_____

_____

_____

_____

_____

_____

_____

_____

_____

_____

_____

_____

_____

_____

_____

_____

_____

_____

_____

_____

_____

_____

_____

_____

EXERCISE #31 – CREATE YOUR VISIONBOARD

Take the time to create a VisionBoard, representing your visualization of your ideal life, and have it somewhere in your house or office where you can see it regularly. Some people choose to also have these images on their fridge... their bathroom mirror... in their wallet...

One of my early visionboards...

An image representing an "endless tunnel" of books

160

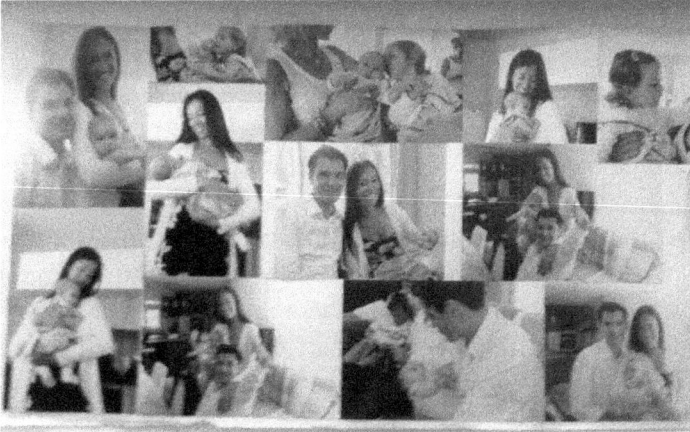

My wife and I created this visionboard of pictures with our two
young nieces, when we were trying for a child, to manifest that outcome.

The Law of Attraction

*"You become what you think about most of the time. Plant thoughts
of good health, and abundance in the garden of your mind. Like
energy attracts like energy... If you are in a positive mood, you tend
to attract positive people, events, and circumstances... and it all
begins with your thoughts. Your thoughts determine your physical
world. If you have predominantly thoughts of lack, fear, or failure...
that is what you are producing in your world. If you have constant
thoughts of abundance, success, and love... that is what you will get
most of. If you are stressed and hectic... your world will be stressed
and hectic... But if you are peaceful and harmonious... life will keep
bringing you things that will make you peaceful and harmonious.
Life is a mirror reflecting back to us what we think. The mind is
producing the physical world around us. Life is not happening 'to'
you. Life is responding to you. Change your thoughts, and your
world will change along with it."*

Justin Perry, The Biggest Secret Of Man

Mind Programming Technique #3: Hypnosis

Hypnosis can be an extremely effective tool in your arsenal for transforming your limiting beliefs. Why? Because hypnosis can bypass your conscious mind and work directly on your subconscious.

I use an 8-minute supraliminal Hypnosis track titled 'Abundance' by the late Dr. Laura De Giorgio. I first used in 2010, at the suggestion of my wife (who happens to be a hypnotherapist), to mentally 'unblock' a large amount of money that was stuck in one of our payment gateways. It worked!

Dr. Laura De Giorgio writes:

> "You will tend to experience the fastest results when working with issues you believe to be possible for you to achieve, you are motivated to achieve, and you expect to achieve. The more often you listen to recordings, the more you saturate your mind with positive ideas, the faster results you will get. For best and fastest results listen to hypnosis recordings once or twice a day and to other types of recordings with affirmations throughout the day or while you're sleeping. <u>Listen to the recording UNTIL you get desired results</u>. Depending on the goals you desire to achieve and challenges you are facing, you may experience instant results or it may take you days or weeks or longer to get the results you desire."

> "Suggestions on subliminal and supraliminal tracks are designed to by-pass your conscious awareness and become impressed directly upon your subconscious mind, so you will not hear them consciously. The best time to listen to hypnosis recordings is just before you go to sleep or at such times during the day when you are naturally more relaxed physically, yet mentally still alert enough to follow the guidance on the recording. A part of your mind is always listening, so you will be programming your subconscious mind even if you drift off to sleep."

The hypnosis MP3 I use personally and that I give to my coaching clients includes the following messages and text:

"You now allow the following suggestions to be deeply impressed upon your subconscious mind and stay with you permanently if you so choose. You accept them as your own.

I live and move and have my being in an ocean of infinite abundance.
My life is filled with miracles.
I am open to the flow of infinite abundance.
I am open to experiencing miracles in my life.
I am one with all abundance.
I am one with all the money in the world.
I allow money to freely circulate in my life just like the air that I breathe.
I am fully present in the now.
My slate is clean now and forever.
I have the power to create anything I ever need through the power of my mind.
All the money I ever need comes to me easily and effortlessly.
Money comes to me from every direction.
My net worth easily reaches one hundred million pounds
Money flows to me easily and effortlessly.
I always have more money than I ever need.
I dedicate my life to serving others, to helping people feel better, and as I do, the whole Universe supports me and takes care of me and all of my needs.
All my needs are now and forever instantly supplied.
My life is full of miracles.
My life is wonderful.
I am deeply grateful for my life.
I live and move and have my being in an ocean of infinite abundance."

Mind Programming Technique #4: Subliminal Messages

A lot of successful people credit using subliminal messages as the secret behind their success. The personal development speaker and entrepreneur Anthony Robbins, with a net worth estimated at over $400 million dollars, explains how he was able to turn his life around from being broke and overweight, in his early twenties:

> "I used subliminal messages to condition my mind, to believe I could succeed, to build energy in my body, and anybody who wants to succeed has got to know it doesn't just happen. You can buy a product, but also with that product, you've got to condition your subconscious mind!"

What he means by 'product' is that people often buy courses—such as a course on real estate investing, or stock market trading, or a business opportunity—with the hope of making more money or 'becoming successful'. But unless you condition your mind for success, chances are it won't "work" for you even if it's the smartest wealth creation strategy in the world. He also adds: "The most powerful force in the human psyche is people's need to stay consistent with their IDENTITY."

For example, if your identity is of someone that doesn't earn more than $2,000 a month, or of someone who "doesn't know how to make a lot of money", well guess what? You will subconsciously do whatever it takes to remain true to that identity, and you will not earn a dime more. If you want to bump up your earnings to, say, $40,000 a month, you first need to make that outcome become a part of your **identity**. By programming your subconscious mind with that outcome, you will begin to feel more comfortable and 'at ease' with the prospect of earning $40,000 a month. Your mind is less likely to resist you or sabotage you.

When someone with a mindset of "I earn $2,000 a month" tries a business opportunity which has the potential to earn them $250,000 to $500,000 a year or more, they very rarely succeed. Dr. John Demartini gives the example of a chiropractor who was running a $200,000-a-year practice and who inherited a $1,000,000-a-year clinic. Within two years, Demartini reports, that million-dollar clinic was generating only $200,000 a year. Why? Because that level of success was the chiropractor's identity.

Earning one million dollars a year was 'unfamiliar' to him and outside his comfort zone. As the British psychologist Marisa Peer once said, *"To succeed at anything you have to make the unfamiliar familiar."*

Tiger Woods's father was a US Army officer with a background in psychology. From the age of 6 Tiger Woods was programmed with subliminal messages every day, feeding his mind a steady diet of positive affirmations intended to create an unshakable confidence. They included subliminal declarations such as: *"I focus and give it my all!"*, *"My will moves mountains!"*, *"I believe in me!"*, and *"I will my own destiny!"*

This technology helped him align his mind to his goals, focus on success, block any negativity out of his mind, and achieve extraordinary levels of success—including a net worth of $500 million dollars.

Tiger Woods Secret To Success – Mind Power

"From the age of 6 Tiger Woods used subliminal messages every day, feeding his mind a steady diet of positive affirmations. This helped him to align his mind to his goals, to focus on success, and block any negativity out of his mind. For peak performance, your mind must be trained to peak condition."

Tiger Woods

I Started Using Subliminals In November 2005

Armed with this insight, I started programming my subconscious mind in September 2005 thanks to subliminal messages using a simple software tool that flashed my affirmations on my computer screen for 1/10th of a second, every 5 seconds.

Whenever I was answering my emails, or writing books, creating PowerPoint presentations, or watching a video online, the message "I Earn $40,000 A Month" would flash on my screen, too fast for my conscious mind to read, or for it to be distracting, but my subconscious was being programmed up to 7,000 TIMES A DAY, with no effort on my part.

Every time the message flashed, a neural pathway was being formed and strengthened in my brain between the concept of "I" (my identity) and the concept of "earning $40,000 a month".

David J. Schwartz, author of The Magic of Thinking Big, wrote:

> "The mind is what the mind is fed. [...] When you BELIEVE something can be done, really believe... your mind will find the ways to do it."

This software allowed me to feed my mind with positive goals, changing my dominant pattern of thinking in the process.

The software simply worked its magic, in the background, reprogramming my identity and my beliefs about myself and about what is possible for me, with zero fuss or effort. Four months later, I earned $43,000, a breakout month for my business. Bizarrely, the final $3,000 sale had to be refunded, and I ended the month... earning exactly $40,000!

The following month I decided to really put the software to the test. I typed into it a new affirmation: "I earn $100,000 a month". I had no idea how I could possibly achieve such a gigantic income, and I didn't even believe it was possible for anyone to earn such an income.

And yet the next month I generated $150,000 in sales. An American speaker asked me to organize and promote his seminar in the UK. I could keep the sales from the event, as he only wanted to use the event to fill places for his subsequent course in London.

"I love this, I can absorb my goals and **reprogram my mind a thousand times a day**, while I sit and read e-mail. **This is brilliant – <u>AND IT WORKS!</u>**"

Dr. Joe Vitale

Thanks to my skills in Internet Marketing, in the space of just five weeks I got 2000 people to register for a free event I was running ("The Mental Game Of Money"), without spending a penny on marketing. Armed with my new mindset, my income exploded to $1,160,000 in 2006, or almost exactly $100,000 a month – a 500% increase year-on-year.

The software had allowed me to program my subconscious mind with a new identity, and transform my dominant pattern of thinking. Hundreds of scientific studies now prove that subliminal messages really work, and that they help people increase their confidence and self-esteem, lose weight permanently, quit smoking and other addictions, learn faster and achieve better academic results, and even—astoundingly—reverse the effects of ageing, help you feel and look younger, gain more energy, increase stamina, and improve athletic performances.

The renowned psychiatrist Dr. Gary Casaccio explains:

> "Often our conscious and unconscious minds are at odds with each due to past programming. It is great to have a tool that works directly on the subconscious mind to reprogram that part of ourselves in order to create alignment and congruency with both parts of our minds to assist us in creating the life, relationships, success, health and happiness that we want."

The subconscious mind is programmed through repetition. It's important to note that when reprogramming our minds on a subconscious level, statements need to be written in the affirmative, as the subconscious mind does not process negatives. Repeat the sentence *"I don't want to be fat anymore"* and the subconscious would only receive the instruction *"I... want... to be fat"*.

Of course, when one factors in an understanding of the spiritual world and Universal Laws (for example, the Law of Attraction), this is merely a reminder that "we get more of who we are."

If your affirmation is "I don't want to be fat anymore", you are aligning yourself vibrationally with the thoughts and mind-patterns of overweight people. The Universe gives you more of "not wanting to be fat".

The thoughts of a fit, healthy individual would be, instead:

> "I am fit, energetic, and powerful... I love and accept myself... I love my healthy body... I love exercising every day... I welcome people closer to me... Being fit and beautiful is important... I eat foods that are good for me... Every day in every way I am healthier and stronger... Exercising every day is fun and easy... I am admired for my health and fitness... My cells enjoy the benefits of maximum nutrition... I hydrate my body regularly with pure water... I choose health... I choose to take loving care of my body..."

Similarly, you wouldn't program your subconscious your mind with "I want success" – the Universe would just give you more of wanting success. Instead, align yourself with the mindset of successful, confident people: "I am successful... I love my life and I am grateful... I attract success effortlessly... Every day in every way I am more and more successful... I am an amazing success... I am a powerful creator... I always make the right decisions..."

Try out my Prosperity Power™ Subliminal Software—it is available for instant download at www.LifeCanBeAwesome.com.

Prosperity Power™ Subliminal Software

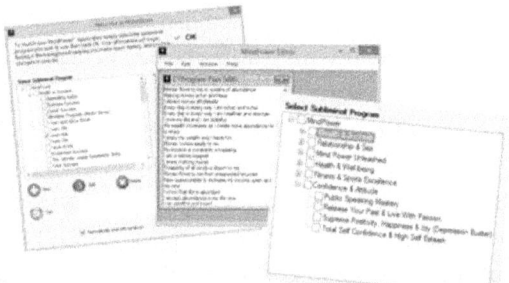

Retail Value $297

Scientific Studies now <u>PROVE</u> that subliminal messages really work and:

❑ Subliminal messages help boost confidence and self-esteem

❑ Subliminal messages help quit smoking, quit drinking, addictions

❑ Subliminal messages help students learn faster, and improve academic results

❑ Subliminal messages help reverse ageing

❑ Subliminal messages improve stamina and athletic performances

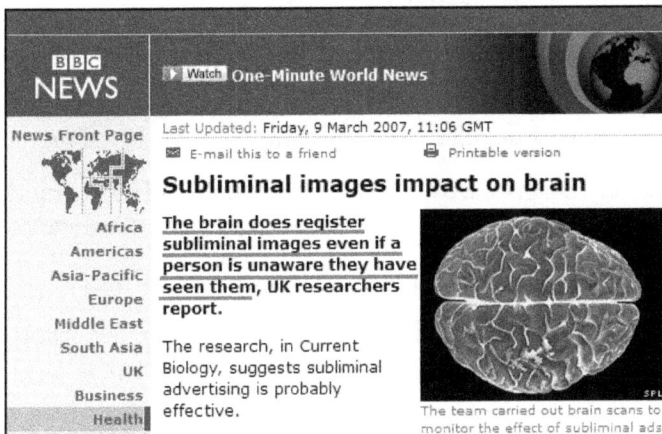

BBC News reports on the power of subliminal images

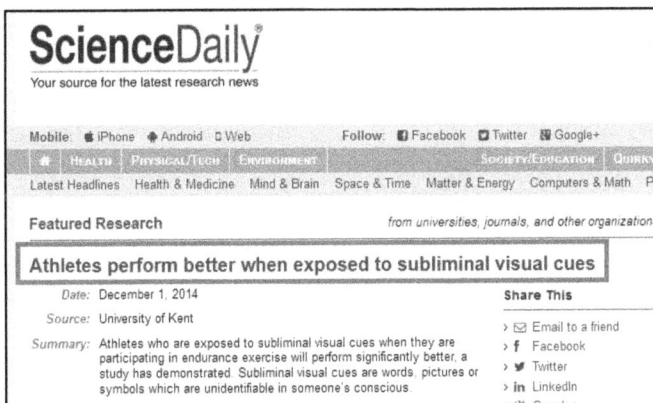

University of Kent study on effect of subliminals on athletic performance

169

The Power of Intention

I understand the power that our thoughts have on our life. This is why I use on a daily basis the practice of conscious intention. Here are a few examples of how I "program" my reality into being:

- ❏ The moment I wake up I set an intention for the day: *"I'm having an amazing day today!"*. You are more likely to have a great day, if you *intend* for it to be so.

- ❏ Before going to sleep, I write down my schedule for the next day. I *intend* for a productive day.

- ❏ I write down my goals. By doing so, they are more likely to manifest in physical reality.

- ❏ I have a detailed, written "Life Vision" describing my ideal life.

- ❏ Years ago I wrote down in detail my 'ideal partner'. As a result, I manifested the woman I am blessed to call my wife.

- ❏ I give thanks for my food, prior to every meal.

- ❏ I say my affirmations out loud every day, including expressing my gratitude for all the love, joy, and abundance in my life.

- ❏ I have the words 'Gratitude', 'Love', 'Peace', 'Joy' taped to our glass bottles and water filter.

- ❏ When I leave for a trip I visualize arriving at my destination on time, safe and sound.

- ❏ When I'm into town I set an intention that the perfect parking space awaits me at my destination. And it does.

- ❏ When I am travelling abroad, I write down a one-page intention of exactly how I want our trip to go, including our safe return home.

- ❏ I write down my intentions prior to attending a meeting or event.

- ❏ Before Mira gave birth to our two girls, we wrote a one-page intention describing how the birth would play out, the drive to

170

the clinic, how the staff would be, how long the labour would last, how she wouldn't need any drugs or medical interventions... Everything happened as intended.

Remember: everything is energy, and this energy is malleable to your thoughts and intention!

EXERCISE #32 – CREATE YOUR DAILY "POWER REGIMEN"

Create and print out a single A4 sheet of paper containing your daily health & fitness routine, your affirmations, and your visualizations. Here is my own "Daily Power Regimen":

MY DAILY POWER REGIMEN

* I start my day with 'Green Juice' for cleansing, alkalizing, energy, and maximum nourishment
* I go for a walk twice a day, and I connect with nature
* I do weight training 3 x per week *(good for BONE DENSITY)* Build up Chest area – empowers m
* 3 litres of water a day. Supplements. I eat organic red meat 3x/week. No sugar, no processed food
* I Program Myself daily with Subliminal Power + 'Abundance' hypnosis mp3

Incantations & affirmations:

* I am a god-guided expression of health, wealth, happiness and joy for myself and all the lives that I have the privilege of touching. All that I want, desire, and need is instantly manifested and flows to me in oceans and oceans of abundance as I continue to create even more abundance for all to enjoy. I am grateful beyond measure and appreciative of all that has already flowed to my team and me.
* I Express Myself Freely and Creatively! I Am Amazing! I Am Inspiration! I Am Power!
* No Matter What I Have Done Or Not Done I Am Worthy Of Love! I Love And Accept Myself
* Money Flows To Me In Avalanches of Abundance, From All Directions, And I Am Grateful Beyond Measure For All The Abundance And Love And JOY In My Life! How Can I Appreciate Even More All The Abundance And LOVE And JOY In My Life Right Now?
* **I Love My Life! I Am Rich, I Am Loved, I Am Grateful!** (I am a Multi-Millionaire!)
* Millions Of Copies Of My Books Are Sold Worldwide, I Inspire Millions of People Around!
* Every Day, In Every Way, I Am Healthier & Stronger! Every Day In Every Way I Am Better & Better!
* Every Day, In Every Way, I Am Richer And Richer! Every Day In Every Way I Am More Efficient & Produc
* I Am a Genius and I Apply My Wisdom! I Am a Master Reader! I Am Efficient And Productive!
* I Have Access To All The Wisdom That I Need. I Am In Alignment Self-Oversoul-God-Mind!
* I Communicate with Oversoul Daily and Release All Up To It (and them up through the crown into the silver infinity)
* I let go of my illusion of abandonment. In True Reality, nothing within God-Mind can ever aban
* I have the total support of my Oversoul and God-Mind with me at all times, wherever I go.
* I am one with my Oversoul family and God-Mind in conscious awareness.
* I use the BROWN MERGER symbol 3 times per day! Place at pineal gland, brain stem, heart chakra:
  "I now merge with all alternate selves in all universes where I exist where I have financial abundance"

Visualization:

* I Visualize **My Perfect Life** and I Celebrate Its Attainment! ☺
* I Visualize around me and throughout me for unconditional love for myself!
* I Visualize in my Thyroid Area *(to unblock my communication)*
* I Visualize ICE BLUE in my Heart Chakra area, blow out Red, Grey, Blue
* I Visualize and breathe in MEDIUM GREEN in every cell of my body!
* I Visualize the POWER ARCHETYPE and the 'Ultimate Protection Technique'
* I Visualize the Chakra Spinning exercise and release work daily *("It will open up your finances!")*
* I Do visualization daily
* I Do visualization daily

Dear God, please put the colour pink inside my body for eternal love. Wrap me in crystals. Paint me gold and paint me silver. Wrap me in mirrors. Place me inside of a pyramid filled with bright white light, so the light goes through the apex of pyramid. And please put me in a suite of shining armour, and send you loving thoughts and prayers to everyone I met, everyone I am meeting, and everyone I will meet. Amen.

YOUR DAILY POWER REGIMEN

My recommendations:

1) Set a time each day to run through your Daily Power Regimen. I use my 'Daily Power Regimen' at 8am and 7pm every day, just before meditating. It takes me approximately 6 minutes to go through my daily affirmations and visualization exercises each time. It is more important that you do this *consistently every day* rather than "doing it perfectly" or "how long you spend on it" each day. Get into the habit.

2) Read your "200 Reasons Why" and your "20 Things I Am Grateful For" once a day; make it a part of your Daily Power Regimen.

3) Add a 'night-time routine' to your Daily Power Regimen. In the evening, before going to bed, <u>plan your day ahead</u> (to maximize your productivity). This involves writing down your schedule for the day ahead. Also, count your blessings (read your 'Gratitude' list, or write down what you are grateful for about today), and write down a 'quality question' (a problem you want your subconscious to work on during the night).

Summary – Chapter 4

❏ Your invisible world creates your visible world.

❏ Your outer world is a reflection of your inner world, and it corresponds to your dominant patterns of thinking. Change your thinking, and you change your life.

❏ You can change your dominant patterns of thinking thanks to Affirmations, Visualization, Hypnosis, and Subliminal Technology.

❏ You become what you think about most of the time. Plant thoughts of good health, and abundance in the garden of your mind. If you have predominantly thoughts of lack, fear, or failure... that is what you are producing in your world

❏ Your thoughts are creative. Positive thoughts create positive outcomes in your life. *"I gave all My spirit children the same power to create which I have as the whole. Our essence is the same... with all the same properties and abilities, including the ability to create physical reality out of thin air."*

❏ Use the great command that calls forth creative power: I AM. Make I-am statements to others. "I am" is the strongest creative statement in the universe.

❏ Affirmations, spoken with feeling (excitement, gratitude, joy), are incredibly powerful in manifesting a desired reality.

❏ The Greek shipping magnate Onassis would rehearse in his head over and over again how he wanted his business meetings to turn out.

❏ According to Abraham-Hicks, 68 seconds of pure thought is equivalent to 2,000,000 action-hours

❏ There are four magical feelings that attract money into your life: GRATITUDE, LOVE, INSPIRATION, ENTHUSIASM. If you are ENTHUSIASTIC about selling your product, your business grows...

❏ The more detail you can envision, the greater your power to create.

❑ To succeed at anything, you have to make the unfamiliar familiar.

❑ The mind is what the mind is fed. When you BELIEVE something can be done, really believe… your mind will find the ways to do it.

❑ The most powerful force in the human psyche is people's need to stay consistent with their IDENTITY. Change your identity—through affirmations, hypnosis, or subliminal messages, for example—and you change your life.

❑ The subconscious mind is programmed through repetition.

CHAPTER 5

Master Your Money

Money doesn't go where it is needed most; it goes where it is appreciated and is managed wisely. To attract more wealth into your life, you need to demonstrate that you can first manage the wealth you already have.

The wealthy do not spend their money in the same way as the poor or middle-class. Most poor or middle-class people try to "keep up with the Joneses" and impress people around them. Sometimes it is out of insecurity, or the need for approval, but whatever the case the result is the same: they spend all they earn *and* they I get into debt. Their liabilities often grow, month after month, as a result of this mindset.

Millionaires, on the other hand, I pay themselves FIRST. The wealthy spend less than they earn, and they invest the difference. The wealthy see money primarily as seeds to be planted that will grow into 'money trees'...

With every dollar I earn, I have a choice. It can become the seed of a money tree... if I put it towards buying an income-producing asset. Your assets and your sources of income tend to multiply, when you adopt this mindset.

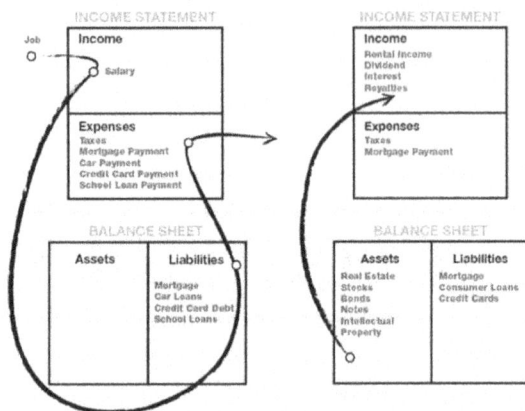

Why The Rich Get Richer: A Virtuous Cycle
(source: *Rich Dad, Poor Dad* by Robert Kiyosaki)

One of my "money trees", by the way, is in the form of 3,000 income-producing books and information products that produce a passive income every day. They help fund my projects and my new businesses. But it could just as well have been 3,000 shares in profitable companies, or 30 apartment blocks. The principle is the same: transform earned income into assets and passive income.

I know a lot of smart people who generate a very good income but don't have much to show for it. Building wealth requires a different skillset to simply "making money". If you don't have the discipline and rigour to spend less than you earn, and then invest those savings wisely, you may have a great lifestyle, but it doesn't mean your wealth is growing.

Our educational system is based on the 19th century Prussian model, designed for creating good soldiers and good factory workers ("Sit down, shut up, and repeat what we tell you! To think is to disobey!"). **We have not been educated about money, wealth creation, wealth management, achieving success, health, and happiness**. We have not been educated about how to create passive income and achieve financial freedom. As a result, most people are not financially savvy, at all. Millions of people are spending their entire lives working in jobs they hate, just to get by.

I wasn't educated about managing my money either. After blowing through a couple of million dollars earned in my first three years in business—it was fun, but not advisable—here's what I started doing:

- ❏ I started living within my means, while saving 50 to 75% of my net income every month. My advice? Find ways to *save money*, and **live within your means**. Start by saving $100 a month... then save $200 a month... and keep increasing how much you save every month, month after month. Maintain a monthly household budget and **document your spending**... it is an excellent way to start taking control over your finances.

- ❏ I kept saving money. This allowed me to invest at the right time in low-risk yet highly profitable opportunities... because I had accumulated enough capital. I also found that **having a decent amount in savings made me feel very abundant and relaxed about money, which attracts even *more* money into one's life** (why? Because the Universe gives you more of who you are...).

- ❏ I kept adding to my income streams, by creating new products.

- ❏ I set a new standard for myself and stuck to it: to always have a minimum of €250,000 in savings.

* * * * * * * * *

A few years ago I found myself waiting in line at an ATM machine at Gatwick airport. I happened to look over the shoulder of the young man in front of me as he checked his balance—he had £257 in his account. He was my age, in his mid-to-late twenties, and was dressed for construction work. I remember the amount because I thought to myself, "that is odd... I have literally one thousand times more in my account... a quarter of a million pounds...".

179

I thought this out of fascination, not arrogance. That moment was seared into my memory because it jolted me—the realization that I could have just as easily be standing in this man's shoes—a working class security guard on minimum wage—had I not followed Balthazar's advice and taken the steps to change my destiny four years earlier.

* * * * * * * *

"What is the fastest and easiest way to make a lot of money?" That is the #1 question I get from people all over the world, due to the success of my first book. This is typical from business opportunity seekers who understand little about business, or money.

I have seen innumerable people go for get-rich-quick schemes only to lose all their money and go right back where they started. If you think you're just going to get rich overnight, or get rich quick with no effort, then you are dealing with high probabilities of losing your money.

I recently received the following email from a man who was interested in attending my 5-day "Millionaire Mind" retreat. I have changed his name to 'Albert Putnell', for reasons you are about to understand. This is a 100% genuine email, I assure you...

> "Hi Mark, I wish I could attend your retreat!! Awaiting news of a large pay-out, but may be another scam. My pensions have been scammed by investing in 'European Fine Wines', who promised to sell my wine collection. The broker told me he'd like to join me in a land deal he'd heard about on the internet. He told me to max out all my credit cards, charged to the land deal—which was the scam set up by his bosses—I lost some £20,000! The CEO was jailed, but police have not been able to trace what happened to the money! Then, 'Capital World Markets' promised me a 7% return per month, which accrued my final pension annuity of £20,000 for some 18 months, reaching £40,000 before the CEO was arrested for "touching up ladies!" My investment disappeared! Many smaller losses have also been experienced, leaving me with no reserves. A recent betting syndicate has supposedly made me £40,000, from the £5,000 I put in, which should be paid out in the next couple

of weeks! (I've only waited 9 months... I've just received a text from the guy -Rojer -handling this, saying "he's in hospital, on an antibiotic drip, has pneumonia! 2nd text says "balance transfer 9th June". 3rd text says "its guaranteed"!). A Chinese fellow has traced an inheritance of millions left by an Albert Putnell with no relatives! He is in the process of finding a bank to handle the transfer to me!! To be split 50/50!!"

Needless to say, Albert never saw that £40,000 pay-out from the betting syndicate, nor a penny of that supposed "inheritance of millions" from China. Some people will go to extraordinary lengths to avoid having to think, create value, or take on the responsibility of managing and investing their money...

And some simply have a subconscious need to get rid of all their money as fast as possible, be it out of guilt or negative neuro-associations.

* * * * * * * *

EXERCISE #33 – MONTHLY BUDGET

What is your monthly household budget?

Rent/mortgage   _____

Bills   _____

Food/shopping   _____

Transport/car   _____

Entertainment/going out   _____

Other   _____

Amount put in savings   _____

TOTAL   _____

What are 7 ways how you can save money right now?

(Be creative and resourceful! Think of how you can create win-win situations, split costs with someone else, reduce your outgoings, live somewhere better and cheaper, barter and exchange services, etc.!)

_____

_____

_____

_____

_____

_____

_____

_____

_____

_____

_____

_____

_____

_____

_____

_____

_____

Pay yourself FIRST!

This is one of the most powerful wealth accumulation processes ever discovered... ALWAYS pay yourself FIRST. What this means, is that every month put money aside to buy income-producing assets, *before* you pay bills, food, rent, ANYTHING.

If you are then pressured to pay the bills, the rent, etc., you WILL find a way to come up with the extra money. The pressure will force you to succeed in doing so. It will require your brain to work harder, and force you to get smarter, bolder, more determined, and more resourceful.

Most people in Western countries spend 10% more than they earn, every month, and go deeper in debt. 70% of Americans don't have any savings—not even $400. Why? Because people tend to raise their lifestyle instead of increasing their *savings*, when they have more income.

A great and simple idea for increasing one's wealth is this: FORCED INCREASED SAVINGS ON A QUARTERLY BASIS. This means *increasing* how much you save per month, every quarter. You can set it up with your bank or with your broker.

For example, you start saving $100 per month. Then, three months later, that increases to saving $150 per month. Then, $200 per month. And on, and on. You will find that this process psychologically "forces" you to increase your income, to make up for that increase in savings! Every time you increase your savings, your income will grow in step.

COMMIT to sticking to your monthly budget, and commit to reaching a specific amount in your SAVINGS account.

Raise Your Standards

Raise your standards, when it comes to your savings. For example, when I started making good money in 2004, I just wanted to be 'free of debt'. I managed to pay off my £7,000 in debt quickly and I was happy to be at 'zero' in my account. I started making $10,000 a month, but still, because I kept increasing my expenses in step with my income, my balance would always go back down to *zero*. Since the standard that I had set in my mind was to 'not be in debt', I simply spent whatever was coming in.

In 2005 I decided to set a new standard: I MUST have £20,000 in savings in my account MINIMUM, at all times. Within two months I made that happen. Because that amount had become my new *standard*, whenever my savings dipped below that figure I quickly did whatever it took to get it above the £20,000 threshold.

I then raised my standards to £50,000. And later, to €120,000... then €250,000...

Because I had made it a *standard* (an absolute MUST), it happened.

What is YOUR new standard?

Your SAVINGS goal: _____

Return *of* capital is more important than Return *on* capital.

Preserving CAPITAL is key – this means investing in safe ways so that you never lose your capital. The probabilities of success are in doing the basics. Don't go for big gambles. Slow and steady wins the game.

> *"If you speculate... it's almost as dangerous if it works than if it doesn't... if it works, you get cocky and take risks."*
>
> *Simon Black, founder of SovereignMan.com*

You hear of people making overnight fortunes in real estate or the stock market... don't be fooled... stay the course... keep working your plan... You can't manage money successfully until you learn to manage your EMOTIONS!

Most people can tolerate up to 10% fluctuation in their net worth without emotion... but anything beyond that, they freak out and overreact. Don't let your greed or your fear sway you.

Don't fall for stock market hucksters. Most investors *suck* at picking stocks and timing their trades. Instead, buy great "value" when you find it. This has a lot to do with becoming knowledgeable about cycles throughout our history… (check out economist Harry Dent).

My mentor Balthazar recommended that I study the investment masters of the past century for three years before I started investing myself. This allows you to have more perspective on the world of investments, and not get swept up into the mass hysteria or popularity of a passing fad.

For example, John Templeton said you make the most amount of money in times of great pessimism. In 1939, just as WWII was starting, he took his savings and borrowed money to get $10,000 together, and he bought all the stocks in the market that were at $1 or less. At the end of WWII he became the first BILLIONAIRE investor who started with only $10,000.

I believe stocks and real estate will become much more affordable after 2022-2026… A global financial crash and even a world war might well set the stage for a 'reset' of the international financial system.

Your job in the meantime is to become "financially vibrant" by building up your brand to benefit from multiple streams of income. This will put you in good stead to take advantage of the huge opportunities coming our way.

Avoid Getting Into Debt

Avoid debt if you can. Debt is a deficit of energy. It is a liability that *costs* you money, month after month. Make sure you live within your means and you spend less than you earn, every month.

People are getting more and more into debt, buying things they don't need, egged on by what John Cummuta calls "The Coalition of Four": Advertisers + Media + Credit Lenders + Merchants.

The media present us with a constant stream of glamorous lifestyles, then advertisers make us feel insecure about what we have, and finally Credit Lenders present us with the lure of "free money"... They've perfected this to the point where they can now sell us anything. They know exactly how to push our buttons. No wonder the difference between what most people earn and what they spend minimal if anything at all. Eventually they get you to spend your entire income. Then come the credit lenders with their promise of *"0%-for-6-months"* credit...

The Coalition is manipulating you. The Coalition has trained you to be a good "consumer". Driven by advertising and popular culture, you desire to buy a big house, a new car, fancy expensive clothes, every new convenience, toy, and fashion. You end up wasting money trying to *look* rich... the problem is, you never actually become rich!

The fact is—as described in the book "The Millionaire Next Door"— most millionaires in the US have a modest house, drive a modest car, and have simply spent less than they earn their entire lives and invested the difference.

Be more creative if you need to raise money: instead of turning to debt, *sell* something, or write a business plan and pitch it to potential investors.

John Demartini gives the following advice for reframing (thinking differently) about what debt is, in order to pay it off more easily:

> "The things you don't feel like paying for—paying off your debt, for example—you will find hard to find the money for. Convert DEBT into 'SERVICE'. Every cheque you send out to pay off your debt, write to them "Thank you for investing in me!" Focus on SERVICE... and Debt disappears!"

He also advises, incidentally, not to loan money to friends or family...

He states:

- ❑ Don't ever loan money to friends or family. 90% never get it back.

- ❑ When you bail people out, they'll never learn.

- ❑ The people you want to rescue... are the parts of you you haven't learned to love and appreciate... You want to help that destitute 15-year old? That's because of how *you* were when you were 15... The second you rescue them, they'll resent you.

- ❑ Don't spend money on *desperation*, don't invest in *desperation*... you'll be investing in a culture of insufficiency. Give your money to people who can order it better than you.

He also makes this interesting—though separate—point about educating your children: *"Educate your children about money. Nowadays, children just expect to get things for no work... You have to teach them to WORK for things! Give them a piggy bank and teach them how money works."*

In my personal experience, if you want to help your loved ones, help them reach self-sufficiency by sharing with them educational resources (business and marketing courses, for example), sending them to a seminar, investing in them, or just give them money as a gift—without expecting it back.

6 Rules For Investing

My friend Simon Black, founder of SovereignMan.com, shares the following six rules for investing. He writes: "One of my value investing mentors explained to me, for instance, that if you're going to invest in the stock market, you should buy a single share as if you're buying the entire business. And he laid out six rules to follow when making any investment...

#1. Always consider the risks before even thinking about how much you can make

Sometimes it's worth taking huge risks where there's a good chance you'll lose everything. Startups are a great example; there was a 95%

chance that Google was going to fail when it first launched. But the return has been more than 100,000x the initial investment. Clearly that kind of return is worth the risk. Know the risk, and make sure the reward is worth it.

#2. Don't invest unless you know WHY

Before making any investment, have an objective. After all, there are a lot of different reasons to invest. Sometimes you might be seeking income, i.e. buying rental real estate for the cash flow. Capital appreciation is another common goal; people are typically looking to turn a $100,000 investment portfolio into $500,000. But there are other reasons as well: Asset protection. Hedging against financial/systemic risks. Reducing taxes. Estate planning. You can even invest to gain citizenship. To accomplish any goal requires careful planning and disciplined execution, whether you're trying to lose weight or save for retirement. But you can't ever create a plan unless you start with a clear objective.

#3. Invest in people of integrity who have a track record of success.

Most investments are 'managed'. Apple is managed by CEO Tim Cook and the Board of Directors. Investments in government bonds are essentially 'managed' by the Treasury Department and all the politicians and bureaucrats. Any investment with dishonest or incompetent management will ultimately become worthless. It's simply a question of time. A great asset managed by competent people of integrity will be a winner.

#4. Buy assets that generate vast amounts of cash flow.

No exceptions. A profitable business (or any asset that produces safe, strong cash flow) makes sense in any environment: inflation, deflation, stagnation, etc.

#5. Avoid excessive debt.

Borrowing can be a good thing, especially when interest rates are low. But too much debt leaves a company (or government) vulnerable and unable to pay its stakeholders.

#6. Know the value of what you're buying, and never overpay for it.

Know exactly what a company is worth. With stocks, for example, you can look at a company's "net tangible assets"; if a company has $1 million in cash, $1 million in inventory, and $500k in debt, then its net tangible assets equal $1.5 million. Buying well-managed, profitable companies that sell near (or even below) the values of their net tangible assets provides a substantial margin of safety. This is a core principle of value investing.

(source: www.sovereignman.com)

* * * * * * * *

EXERCISE #34 – TRACK YOUR INCOME & EXPENSES

On the 1st of every month, write down in an Excel spreadsheet, or on sheet of A4 paper that you keep on file, **how much you spent in the previous month** (and what you spent it on), and **how much you earned** (broken down into income streams). Separate your expenses into PERSONAL expenses (utility bills, food & shopping, entertainment & going out, holidays, car & transport, purchases) and BUSINESS expenses (e.g. staff, marketing, web services, etc.).

How much did you spend in the previous month? What did you spend it on?

_____

_____

_____

_____

_____

_____

_____

_____

_____

_____

_____

How much did you earn in the previous month? What are your income streams?

_____

_____

_____

_____

_____

_____

_____

_____

Summary – Chapter 5

❏ Money doesn't go where it is needed most; it goes where it is appreciated and is managed wisely.

❏ To attract more wealth into your life, you need to demonstrate that you can first manage the wealth you already have.

❏ The wealthy spend less than they earn and invest the difference.

❏ The wealthy see money primarily as seeds to be planted that will grow into 'money trees'.

❏ With every dollar you earn, you have a choice. It can become the seed of a money tree, by putting it towards buying an income-producing asset.

❏ Millionaires pay themselves first. Every month put money aside to buy income-producing assets before you pay anything else.

❏ Our educational system is based on the 19th century Prussian model, designed for creating good soldiers and good factory workers. We have not been educated about how to create passive income and achieve financial freedom. As a result, most people are not financially savvy, at all.

❏ Find ways to save money, and live within your means. Start by saving $100 a month, and keep increasing how much you save every month, in order to accumulate capital.

❏ A great and simple idea for increasing one's wealth is this: forced increased savings on a quarterly basis (every three months *increase* the amount you are saving).

❏ Having savings attracts even more money into one's life because of the Law of Attraction.

❏ Raise your standards. Set a new standard for how much money you MUST have in your savings, and never allow it to dip below that amount.

❏ Return of capital is more important than Return *on* capital.

- ❑ The probabilities of success are in doing the basics. Don't go for big gambles. Slow and steady wins the game.

- ❑ Study the investment masters of the past century for three years before starting to invest.

- ❑ According to John Templeton, you make the most amount of money in times of great pessimism.

- ❑ Be more creative if you need to raise money: instead of turning to debt, sell something, or write a business plan and pitch it to potential investors.

- ❑ Before making any investment, have an objective.

- ❑ Invest in people of integrity who have a track record of success.

- ❑ Buy assets that generate vast amounts of cash flow.
  Know the value of what you're buying, and never overpay for it.

- ❑ People are getting more and more into debt, buying things they don't need, egged on by Advertisers + Media + Credit Lenders.

- ❑ Avoid debt if you can. Debt is a deficit of energy. It is a liability that costs you money, month after month.

- ❑ Most millionaires in the US have a modest house, drive a modest car, and have simply spent less than they earn their entire lives and invested the difference.

EPILOGUE

Shortly after completing the exercises I met up again with Balthazar at his mansion, on a windy day in November. He seemed preoccupied, but I hardly noticed. I was too excited. I couldn't wait to tell him the news.

"I did the exercises, you know... every one of them... and it's working! Things have started to change! I've started making money online!", I blurted out.

"Well done. Only a handful of people ever show the fortitude to take on these exercises, let alone go through with them to the end. Frankly, I didn't think you would. I am pleasantly surprised," Balthazar said, approvingly.

I explained to him how I had kept learning new things, since our last meeting, especially about marketing and how to SELL.

"That is a vital skill to have. But you know, income follows ASSETS. In the long run, you will need a different set of skills. You will need to learn how to create a SYSTEM and how to build a TEAM," he continued, as he outlined a roadmap for taking my business to the next level.

But those are lessons for another time. :)

* * * * * * * *

FINAL THOUGHTS

What is money, really, when all is said and done? It is a tool for magnifying your impact. A tool that can open doors for you, provide you with more leverage, more opportunities, and more choice; the choice to live life at the highest level possible. There's nothing but LIMITLESS POTENTIAL ahead of you.

It's never a question of CAN you do it, but rather WILL you do it. It comes down to your level of desire, hunger, and a willingness to overcome your FEARS by confidently taking positive steps every day towards achieving your dreams.

Don't tell yourself the lie that "you can't do it". The truth is you CAN but you have been afraid! Well, it's time to kick those fears to the curb, think BIG, unleash your potential, and create a *magnificent* life!

The secret is… If money was where you thought it was all these years… you'd be rich already. The truth is that what you have always wanted is inside of you. Wealth, abundance, 'being rich' … is merely a state of being. A way of thinking.

And yes, you do need some training and some skills. This is why I invite you to take the next step on your journey to success **today**, by signing up for our live events or coaching programs. Keep developing your mindset. Surround yourself with successful people. Ultimately, your business only grows in proportion to how much *you* grow.

You Are Loved And Cherished Forever

The world is merely a stage, for us to have fun and be fully self-expressed. Let us bring awareness and love to more people. Let us heal their hearts, their minds, and their bodies.

Take advantage of this incredible opportunity to be alive.

Truly live with passion. Create a magnificent life. And remember...

You are loved and cherished, forever.

You have nothing to fear.

There is nothing you can do wrong.

Get in touch!

Feel free to send in your thoughts about this book or about anything else by emailing us at info@prosperitypower.com.

If you are interested in attending one of our live seminars, or joining us on one of our retreats, visit www.LifeCanBeAwesome.com.

We look forward to hearing from you soon and meeting you in person at one of our live events!

To Your Happiness & Success,

Mark Anastasi

NEXT STEPS

I invite you to purchase and download the complete "Unleash The Millionaire Within" audio and video course, together with the **Prosperity Power™ software**, and get $3,482 worth of bonuses for FREE, at www.LifeCanBeAwesome.com.

I also invite you to attend our live retreats and seminars, and join our monthly group coaching program titled **The Prosperity Club**, also available at www.LifeCanBeAwesome.com.

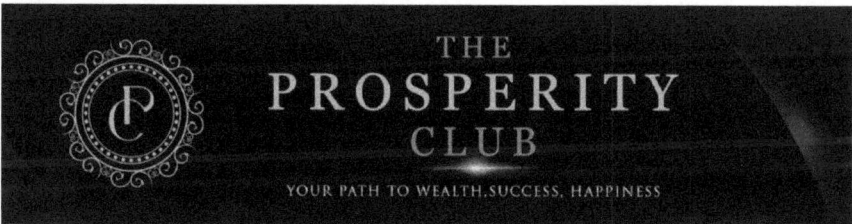

Never, Ever, Ever Give Up

"My strategy in life is simple: I make up for a profound lack of talent by refusing to quit. That's enabled me to accomplish almost every goal I've set for myself — from winning a high school state championship in water polo (when I joined the team I had to play goalie because I could barely swim)... to achieving academic goals (I must be one of the few people with dyslexia to pursue a career as a writer)... to building relationships (my wife broke up with me six times)... to building this business (early in my career my business partner, called me "hopeless"). It's amazing what you can accomplish if you simply refuse to quit."

Porter Stansberry, founder of
Stansberry Research International

"Success seems to be connected with action. Successful people keep moving. They make mistakes, but they don't quit."

Conrad Hilton

"Most people give up just when they're about to achieve success. They quit on the one-yard line. They give up at the last minute of the game, one foot from a winning touchdown."

Ross Perot, billionaire founder of EDS

SUCCESS STORIES

I have had the great privilege of sharing my insights and ideas with audiences all over the world, through the written word as well as via seminars. As a result, people have sent in hundreds of wonderful messages of how they managed to turn their life around—here are a few excerpts from some of them.

"My income literally SOARED within a few weeks of attending your seminar!"

"My income literally SOARED within a few weeks of attending your seminar! I made over $200k in the first year, and $700k in my second year. I have earned millions of dollars since! :)) Thanks Mark!" – Shaqir Hussyin

"I Make $30,000 To $50,000 A Month Thanks To What I Learned At Your Seminar!"

Hey Mark, just wanted to let you know, thanks to what I learned at your seminar I am now making $30,000 to $50,000 a month thanks to totally free online traffic!" – Jem

"I Am Now Pulling $200,000 A Month!"

"Hi Mark, thank you very much for the idea and the motivation from the call we had. I built out a $5k high ticket offer and my team is now pulling in $200k a month selling this on the phone!" – Lee McIntyre

"I Make £30,000 A Month On Autopilot Thanks To What I Learned At Your Seminar!"

"Thank you Mark. I made my first sale within 4 days of your seminar, and since the time we spoke last time I almost tripled my monthly earnings. I am now making £30,000 per month on autopilot, providing internet marketing services to businesses." – Dominica Alicia

"I Earned $1,000,000 Last Year After Attending Your Seminar!"

"If it wasn't for Mark Anastasi I wouldn't be where I am today. Who you can be when you break through is Limitless." – Aaron Darko

"I Get $50,000 A Month In Recurring Income! I Love Your Work!"

"Hi Mark, I am very happy with attending your seminar, after reading your book. Thanks for the business plan! You showed me how to create a system. I now get $50,000 a month in recurring income! I love your work!" – Mark Ryan

"I Made $2,500,000 In 4 Months After Attending Your Seminar!"

"I attended your SpeedCash seminar in London and you introduced me to your software developer. After partnering with him I made $2.5m in just 4 months by selling the software worldwide thanks to joint venture webinars! Thank you!" – Tom H.

"I Now Make $30,000 A Month
After Attending Your Seminar!"

"Hi Mark, thank you for having me on your coaching program! I'm now making $30,000 a month from selling ebooks on Kindle! My outsources do the work, and I sell them all day long thanks to Amazon. :))" – Irma B.

"Thanks to your Marketing Bootcamp I Made
An Extra £250,000 In 6 Months!"

"Mark Anastasi and his Millionaire Marketing strategies have just made me an extra £250,000. As a direct result of attending this incredible seminar Mark uncovered hidden assets and profit busting opportunities within my business. I can't recommend this course enough." – Neil Asher

"Thanks To Mark I Gave Up My Job
And Now Make A Full-time Living Online!"

"Mark's course was superb. The information, contacts and ideas that he shared that weekend were inspiring, cutting edge, visionary, extremely generous and complete. He's the genuine article and clearly wants to contribute. His passion is contagious and it's clear that he truly wants to help inspire and empower people by giving them the tools and tips that they need." – Ben Brophy

"I Make $15,000 to $20,000 A Month thanks to
What You Shared With Me At Your Seminars!"

"Thank you Mark for all that you shared with me at your many seminars. I tried what you said and I now make $15,000 to $20,000 a month thanks to Facebook marketing, CPA marketing, and mobile marketing!" – Alusine Sesay

"I Make $500,000 A Year Thanks To What I Learned At Your Seminar!"

"Hi Mark, I've been flying over from Norway to come see your last four seminars. It's life changing. I now have 20 clients, paying me $1,700 to $10,000 a month, bringing in more than $500,000 a year." – Rune Johansen, Norway

"We Now Have Clients In 7 Countries! Thank You!"

"Thank you Mark for the seminar. You opened my eyes to the endless possibilities for creating wealth. Our company has simply exploded since we last met. We have clients now in 7 countries as well as subsidiaries in India and Lithuania, after you showed me how at the Summit. I can't thank you enough!" – Mark Donnan

"I Made More Than $3,000,000 After Attending Your Seminar!"

"Thank you for your seminar in London. One year later my business now generates more than $3,000,000 a year!" – Kieran Gill

"I Earned More Than $1,000,000 Working From Home After Attending Your Workshop!"

"Hi Mark, I came to one of your first ever seminars, with my friend Kish. I quit my job and started an Internet-based business… the rest is history!" – Kunjal K.

"I Went From Massive Debt To Massive Success And Financial Freedom!"

"Hi Mark, I started making money within 3 days of attending your seminar, and I now make £5,000 a month in passive income!" – Nigel Daura

"I Make Over $50,000 A Month Thanks To What I Learned At Your Seminar!"

"Hi Mark, thank you for all your coaching in the last year. I now have multiple streams of income, and I bought the house and the Aston Martin car I always wanted!"– Mili Ponce

"I went from ZERO to making $14,000 a month… in just 4 MONTHS!"

"Hi Mark, I was a roofer in the construction industry, until I had an accident at work where I fell through the roof and injured my back. After attending your seminar I went from earning $0 to over $400 per day thanks to Internet Marketing!" – Ben Brooks

"I Make $50,000 A Month In Recurring Income!"

"Thank you Mark. After attending your seminar I started making $50,000 a month in recurring income thanks to my horseracing website!" – Matt Watson

"I Have Made More Than $1,000,000 Thanks To Your Seminar"

"Hi Mark. I made my first few sales online DURING your seminar, and I made $50,000 in my first 7 months online. I have since made well over $1,000,000 from my business. Thank you!" – Paul O'Mahony

"I Earn More Than $10,000 A Month Working Just 2 Hours A Day!"

"Hello Mark, so many things have happened in the last year since I attended your seminar. I now make $10,000 a month thanks to the Internet, working just 2 hours a day writing my newsletter. This is fantastic!" – Ryan H.

"I Now Have My Own 6-Figure-a-Year Business!"

"Hi Mark, thank you for inspiring me at your seminar! I now have my own 6-figure-a-year business!" – Matija B.

Appendix – Rich Thinking vs Poor Thinking

Here are 21 ways how the rich think differently to the poor and middle class...

1) "Life happens to me... I'm a victim...' I blame, complain, justify... I DRUG myself with TV, food, alcohol, drugs... so as not to have to think about my life..." vs "I create my life! I accept total responsibility for everything I have manifested in my life, the good and the bad!"

2) "I don't know what I want... I'm not sure..." vs "I know exactly what I want! I have clear, compelling, written goals. Clarity is power!"

3) "I hope I'll win the lottery..." vs "I make things happen! I create my life with my thoughts! I determine what happens in my life!"

4) "I want to be able to pay the bills... I play the money game to not lose..." vs "I Am COMMITTED to Being Rich! I am committed to adding massive value and creating massive wealth. I think BIG! I play the money game to win!

5) "If I have a lot of money... I'll be judged, I won't be loved, I might fail in business, I might lose it all... it's stressful..." vs "Having a lot of money gives me choices, freedom, the opportunity to contribute more, live out my dreams, and fulfil my potential!" "The more money I make the more I can contribute to the world & my loved ones, and therefore the more LOVE I receive!"

6) "I resent rich and successful people. Rich people are evil, exploitative, selfish..." vs "I admire other honest, successful, entrepreneurial people! I BLESS their wealth & success!"

7) "Having a lot of money turns people into jerks..." vs "Lack does not bring out the best in people. When people feel they don't have enough, when they are in lack, they resort to crime, drugs, and taking advantage of other people in order to survive... The

wealthier I become, the more I can contribute to the world, and my loved ones."

8) "Money Is The Root of All Evil..." vs "Money Is Nothing But The Measure of The Value You Create For Other People!" "The more people I serve, the more people I help, the more people I solve problems for... the wealthier I am."

9) "My boss should pay me more. I shouldn't be working so hard..." vs "How Can I ADD MORE VALUE to my employer and our clients? How can I SERVE more people? How can I solve MORE problems for people?" "What can I GIVE? The more I give, the more I get."

10) "Money is not that important... I'm not interested in money... Money doesn't matter to me..." vs "Having money is EXTREMELY important! Having money equals freedom, choices, opportunities, health, self-improvement, contribution, and much, much more! (And besides... if money is not that important to you... why do you get up and go to a job that you hate for 40+ years of your life?! Just for the heck of it?)

11) "I'm not smart enough to succeed... I don't know how to set up a business..." vs "I can LEARN anything I need to learn. I can HIRE people who know how to do things. I can ask people for advice. I can seek out MENTORS to show me & teach me what I need to know!"

12) "Oh well, I could never do THAT. 'They' are special, 'they' have talent, 'they' are clever..." vs "Anything THEY can do, I can do! Anything anyone has ever achieved, I can MODEL IT and do it too!"

13) "Starting a business is risky... It's safer to work in a JOB." vs "Being an employee means that someone else is in control of your life, you are dependent on a single source of income, and you could get fired at any moment. That's EXTREMELY risky!

14) "Money can't buy you happiness..." vs "Money Gives Me The Freedom And Time To Do The Things I Love!"

15) "You can't be spiritual AND rich." "It is a sin to be rich... Rich people are evil!" vs "Being abundant means being connected to SOURCE. The Universe WANTS us to be abundant and joyful. Anything we want we can manifest. There is nothing spiritual about poverty. It is a SIN to be poor, because being poor means not serving many people and not fulfilling your potential!"

16) "I resent selling, salespeople, marketing..." vs "I Am Willing To Promote Myself and My Value To The Customers Who Need My Products!" "Money Is Nothing But The Measure Of The Value I Create For People, But How Can I Deliver This Value If I Don't Actively Go Out To Reach Them?"

17) "I cannot handle problems... I focus on the scary obstacles and limitations..." vs "I Am Bigger Than Any Problem! Problems are an opportunity for me to grow my comfort zone! Problems are the GYM where I sculpt my character! I Focus On Opportunities & Solutions!"

18) "I'd rather be TOLD what to do..." (Intellectual laziness). I would rather not have to THINK..." vs "I Exercise My Mind! I brainstorm. I THINK my way to wealth. I unlock my inborn creativity! I brainstorm 100 Ways To Add Value & Create Wealth!"

19) "Go to school, get an education, and get a good JOB!" vs "Get a REAL EDUCATION: Learn how to build businesses, how to invest, and train yourself in sales and marketing!"

20) "I can't afford it..." vs "How Can I Afford It?" "I can't..." vs "HOW can I...?"

21) "I work hard for my money..." vs "My money works for ME!"

Appendix – How To Win The Game of Life

Deep down we all know the secrets to a life well lived. The first and obvious step to winning the game of life is… you must learn to love yourself.

- ❑ Learn to **love and accept yourself** *completely*; You are worthy of love. You *are* love. This is the fundamental first step.

- ❑ **Take full responsibility** for your thoughts, choices, and actions in your Life. You are the creator of your reality. If you don't like what you've manifested so far, create something else.

- ❑ You build *esteem for oneself* by being true to yourself, **following your heart**, being **disciplined**, and doing what others are unwilling to do.

- ❑ **Do what you love**, don't just chase after the money.

- ❑ You get to **create your life**, with your thoughts, so be crystal clear about what you really want out of life. That is how your life gets to take off. Write down your goals and a detailed vision of what your ideal life looks like. **Know exactly what you want**, and focus only on what you want.

- ❑ **Allow yourself to be happy**. At least once a week, do something you really enjoy.

- ❑ **Be in the now**; tune into nature; get in the garden and plant trees, vegetables, and flowers… appreciate **all the beauty in the natural world** around you. Appreciate every moment and **savour the gift that is Life**.

- ❑ **Be grateful**, no matter what happens; know that there is divine perfection and a greater plan, and everything that happens serves you in some way. Write in your *gratitude journal* or remind yourself of what you are grateful for at the end of each day. To those who are grateful, more is given.

- ❏ **Surround yourself with positive, happy people**. You become who you spend time with. Spend time with your friends. Help them. Organize fun activities, days out, trips, parties, excursions, get-togethers, barbecues, birthday parties, etc. Don't be isolated; share your feelings with the people close to you.

- ❏ **Stay in touch with your friends**. Build your ties with your community.

- ❏ **Meditate** for twenty minutes every day.

- ❏ **Take care of your body and your health**; exercise and stretch, daily. Move your body! Go out for a walk. Go swimming. Dance. Go to sleep early, and get enough rest. Don't eat junk food; avoid alcohol and drugs (they *worsen* depression); avoid sugar (it wreaks havoc on a person's emotional states).

- ❏ Demonstrate **integrity** in everything you do. Incompletions, lies, deceptions, and avoiding to deal with issues lowers your energy.

- ❏ **Live your life from a place of LOVE,** rather than a place of Fear or Ego... Give more. Help people. Show love and compassion for others. Giving is the path to happiness.

- ❏ At the critical juncture in all human relationships, ask yourself: **"What would LOVE do now?"** No other question is relevant, no other question is meaningful, no other question has any importance to your soul.

- ❏ **Simplify your life.** De-clutter your space and de-clutter your life.

- ❏ **Avoid complaining.** Take on the Will Bowen's 21-day 'no complaining' challenge. *"Complaining focuses you on what's missing. Studies show that the more we complain the more upset and the less happy we become! And we get OTHER people around us upset as well, which adds fuel to our own fire, keeping us upset LONGER!"* – Will Bowen

- ❏ **Live in a place that makes you happy.** Does where you live suit your vibrational frequency? Are there things or people in your living environment that irritate you or drain you of energy?

- ❑ Surround yourself with beautiful things, where you live; **beauty is uplifting** to the soul.

- ❑ **Learn and grow your whole life**. Attend seminars. Invest in yourself. Everything in the Universe is either growing or decaying. Happiness comes from progress. To be happy you need to feel like you are growing and progressing. *Progress = growth = feeling alive = happiness!*

- ❑ Be fully self-expressed creatively. Write a book. Become a speaker. Create music. Create art. Ask a depressed person *"When did you stop creating?"* and see them light up! You are a creator. So, *start creating again.*

- ❑ **Let go of the past**. Let go of guilt. Let go of your regret about the past.

- ❑ **Don't go onto social media**, or only check it once a week.

- ❑ **Don't watch TV.**

- ❑ **Don't read the news.** It is negative, consists of mostly lies and propaganda, and detracts your focus from what you want.

- ❑ Take control of your life by using **the creative power of your mind**; brainstorm solutions. Visualize your ideal outcome.

- ❑ **Every day focus on positive things** and remind yourself of what you are grateful for, what you are proud of, and your compelling goals and vision for the future.

- ❑ Get in **the sun**. Sufficient Vitamin D can prevent depression.

- ❑ Express your true feelings. Don't repress your emotions.

- ❑ **Don't work so hard.** Spend time with your loved ones. No one at the end of their life wishes they'd spent more time in the office.

www.ingramcontent.com/pod-product-compliance
Lightning Source LLC
Chambersburg PA
CBHW061041110426

42740CB00050B/2675